POSTCARDS
OF THE
EASTER RISING

EDWARD
MARGIOTTA

To Tony Best Wishes Edward

Stenlake Publishing Ltd.

This book is dedicated to

Joan Ann Margiotta
My Wife
1942-1998

and

Pauline Mary de Grussa
My Cousin
1946-1999

Text © Edward Margiotta, 2015.
First published in the United Kingdom, 2015,
by Stenlake Publishing Ltd.
Telephone: 01290 551122
www.stenlake.co.uk

ISBN 9781840336931

The publishers regret that they cannot supply copies of any pictures featured in this book.

Contents

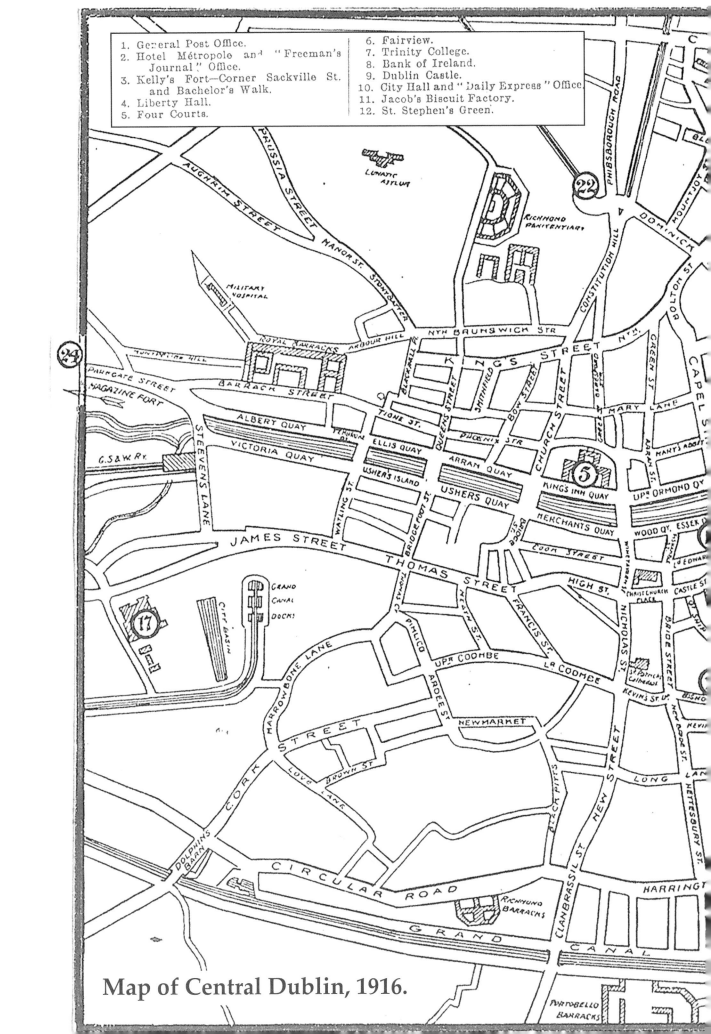

1. General Post Office.
2. Hotel Métropole and "Freeman's Journal" Office.
3. Kelly's Fort—Corner Sackville St. and Bachelor's Walk.
4. Liberty Hall.
5. Four Courts.
6. Fairview.
7. Trinity College.
8. Bank of Ireland.
9. Dublin Castle.
10. City Hall and "Daily Express" Office.
11. Jacob's Biscuit Factory.
12. St. Stephen's Green.

Map of Central Dublin, 1916.

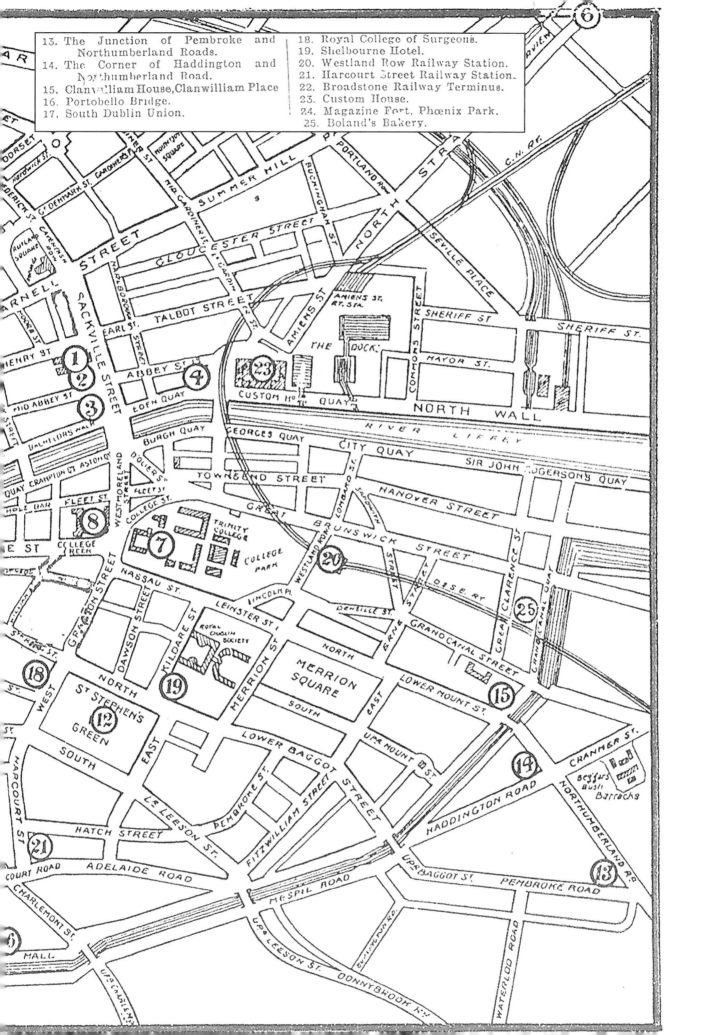

13. The Junction of Pembroke and Northumberland Roads.
14. The Corner of Haddington and Northumberland Road.
15. Clanwilliam House, Clanwilliam Place
16. Portobello Bridge.
17. South Dublin Union.
18. Royal College of Surgeons.
19. Shelbourne Hotel.
20. Westland Row Railway Station.
21. Harcourt Street Railway Station.
22. Broadstone Railway Terminus.
23. Custom House.
24. Magazine Fort, Phœnix Park.
25. Boland's Bakery.

Foreword

I am not a lover of long forewords, so I will try and be brief.

This book has gone through several stages. Initially it was meant to be a checklist or catalogue for deltiologists, postcard collectors to you and me, who collect postcards on the subject of the Easter Rising in 1916, in much the same way as that of a stamp catalogue. It was then expanded into a photographic listing that included information about the images of the people and views displayed on the postcards.

The book now takes the form of a narrative about the Easter Rising, liberally illustrated with original postcards of the period. If some of the postcards shown appear battered and bruised it is because these cardboard images will be a hundred years old in 2016.

Postcard collecting is not an exact science but as with most things in life experience is a great teacher. I am aware that there are many other postcards "out there" that are in the hands of collectors or dealers and this book does not even show all of my collection so the search goes on. Between the covers of this book the postcards displayed cover the most turbulent years of Ireland's history, the Easter Rising, the War of Independence and the Civil War – the latter being the most violent, definitely the most divisive conflict of them all. It may surprise many that postcards were issued on these topics but the period from the turn of the century until the 1930s was described as the "Golden Age of Postcards" when there was no event, no matter how small that was not published in postcard form.

The original book, all but finished, lay dormant for many years. When questioned about it by family and friends I always made promises that I would get down to it and find a publisher. This, of course I never did. About two years ago my daughter-in-law Samantha politely suggested that I finally do something about it. So I wrote off to several publishers without any success and then at a postcard fair in Belfast I met Richard Stenlake of Stenlake Publishing and with his encouragement I set about preparing the book for publication.

In the main the words and images are all mine but I have been very fortunate to have had the help and support of four women in bringing this book to publication: My wife Joan who in the early stages of the book put up with me at, as she called it "my devotions", my cousin Pauline who spent many hours editing the original script, Dr. Mary Clarke of the Dublin City Archives who answered so many of my inane and trivial questions with such good grace and finally my daughter Alexis who has poured over "the homework" that I sent her in order to make this book readable.

I hope you did not find this foreword too long or boring and enjoy the following pages.

Edward Margiotta
London, May, 2015.

Chapter 1: Arms Race

On Sunday 26th July 1914, the yacht *Asgard* arrived at the harbour at Howth, north of Dublin. On board was a cargo of arms amounting to 900 rifles including Mausers and Martinis together with 29,000 rounds of ammunition.

The *Asgard*, whose name means "Land of the Gods" in Norse, was a wedding gift to Erskine Childers and his wife Molly from his American parents-in-law.

Two other yachts, the *Chotah* owned by Sir Thomas Miles and the *Kelpie* owned by Conor O'Brien, were also involved in the movement of the arms. During the off-loading of arms from the *Chotah* to the *Kelpie* the latter broke down, but the *Chotah* made for Howth arriving on the 26th along with the *Asgard* (five days later, on 1st August, the *Kelpie* reached Kilcoolie, Co. Wexford where she was met by a delegation of Volunteers). At Howth waiting to unload the arms was a detachment of Volunteers who had gathered, it is believed, at Croydon Park, Marino before marching off to Howth to collect the arms. The Volunteers had previously paraded through the streets of Dublin in small units in order not to alert the authorities, but the success of gun running at Howth proved that they were a well organised body of men.

Volunteers from Howth moved the guns into Dublin, but at Clontarf a group of the Volunteers were stopped by the Dublin Metropolitan Police (DMP), backed up by a regiment of the King's Own Scottish Borderers (KOSB). Returning to Dublin the KOSB, on reaching Bachelors Walk, were verbally abused and stoned, and the order was given to halt and face the mob. A shot rang out and in reaction the soldiers fired into the crowd, killing three and wounding 40 others. Captain Judge was one of those wounded in the Bachelors Walk Massacre. The subsequent Commission condemned the shooting by the military, which caused indignation throughout the land.

The landing of the arms at Howth was a direct response to the landing of arms at Larne, Donaghadee and Bangor in Northern Ireland on the night of 24th April 1914. Without the tacit agreement of the Ulster authorities and their turning a blind eye to the unloading of 216 tonnes of arms, which included 35,000 rifles 5,000,000 rounds of ammunition and several machine guns, the gun running would never have taken place. All was bound for the Ulster Defence Force (U.D.F.) in their efforts to impress the government that they intended to use all force at their disposal to stop the Third Home Rule Bill.

This postcard of the period shows the landing site of the arms at Howth Harbour.

Communication is part of a good army. Here the bicycle brigade, some with slouch hat, none in uniform, prepare to move off for Howth.

The National Volunteers.
1st & 2nd Battalions, Signalling Company.

This group of men, posing before the Restaurant and Pavilion, are those that were depicted as "A Cyclist Company" on the card on the facing page.

The National Volunteers. "Ireland United is all that we ask"

The men prepare to move off, without arms.

The National Volunteers. Group of Commanders.

Irish National Volunteers. Motor Scout

This view of officers parading for inspection are: Robert Monteith in military uniform, seen writing in a note pad; Mr. C.J. Bodkin, the Volunteers' chief inspector in the dark suit and trilby and Edward Daly in the light trilby. Next to Daly is Captain M. Judge. Following on from left to right are Captains Kerrigan, MacDonagh, Magee and Lenihan.

This scout, with goggles, bandolier and puttees, is ready for action. His bike is a lightweight 2 ½ hp (299cc.) Singer made in Coventry.

BRAVO, ULSTER VOLUNTEERS! The "Mountjoy" unloading "the stuff" at Larne Harbour.

BRAVO, ULSTER VOLUNTEERS! The Gun Runners on the road to Belfast from Larne.

These two cards depict the unloading of arms for the U.D.F. on 24th April 1914. As the event took place at night there were no photographic postcards. All the cards on this subject are therefore artistic impressions.

Chapter 2: The Easter Rising

Ireland was now a military camp with three armies: the British Army, the legitimate army; the U.D.F., the army of Ulster led by Sir Edward Carson, the Dublin-born lawyer and politician; and the Irish Volunteers, the army of the Nationalists led by Eoin MacNeill. The Nationalists would fight for the right to form an independent Irish nation, the U.D.F. would fight to remain in the United Kingdom. Both would initially fail in their objectives, the Easter Rising of the Nationalists would be put down and the Third Home Rule Bill would be passed. Ultimately, however, both would be successful because the Third Home Rule Bill would not be enacted and the Nationalists would gain an independent but divided Ireland.

Patrick Pearse, a barrister and Republican is quoted as saying "There is only one thing more ridiculous than an Ulsterman with a gun and that is a Nationalist without one". This statement, together with Eoin MacNeill's article *The North Began*, led to Bulmer Hobson, a Belfast born Nationalist and member of the secret Irish Republican Brotherhood (I.R.B.) and others to organise a public meeting that was held at the Rotunda in Dublin on 25th November 1913. It was at this meeting that the Irish Volunteers were proposed and formed with MacNeill as its Chief of Staff. The meeting attracted many Irish interest associations including the I.R.B. whose members secured positions on its executive committee.

The rapid growth in the membership of the Volunteers drew it to the attention of John Redmond, the leader of the Irish Parliamentary Party who, perceiving a threat to his power and aim of Home Rule, demanded half of the seats on the Volunteers' executive committee. The I.R.B. members on the committee refused his demands and the movement split with the larger part following Redmond and renaming itself the National Volunteers. The remainder of about 11,000, under the leadership of MacNeill, but under the control of the I.R.B. retained the name Irish Volunteers and went on to fight for an Irish Republic.

From the latter half of the 19th century there was a surge of nationalism across Europe, with the unification of Italy in 1870 and of Germany in 1871. These stirrings came some years later to Ireland: the Gaelic Athletic Association was formed in 1884, the Gaelic League in 1893 and twelve years later in 1905 Sinn Fein was formed.

These Irish associations inspired a feeling of Irishness that had been missing for several generations and as a result created a small but vociferous anti-British voice that was to grow in strength in the years that followed. In 1913 Eoin MacNeill, the Irish historian wrote an article *The North Began* in the newspaper *An Claideamh Soluis* (The Sword of Light), which proposed that the Nationalists should have a force similar to that of the U.D.F.

The Irish Volunteers now structured themselves into an efficient military unit with their committee under the control of the I.R.B.'s secret military council. Thomas Clarke and Sean MacDermott, two of the main I.R.B. leaders, continued to preach for an independent Ireland that would if necessary be achieved by an armed uprising.

Nationalists always considered that the best time to strike against England was when she had problems elsewhere. The First World War was a drain on England's men and resources. For generations Ireland had been a passive neighbour and not since the Young Ireland movement of 1848 had there been any form of serious unrest.

The Volunteers were now openly drilling in cities and towns and buying uniforms from Dublin outfitters. They were in effect an army without arms. To solve this problem they turned to Germany who was initially keen to support any action that would cause a revolution in England's back yard. Darrell Figgis, the author and Sinn Fein politician, and Sir Roger Casement went to Germany to purchase the arms that were eventually landed at Howth. Casement had served the British Government honourably for many years, earning a knighthood for his work on the plight of indigenous peoples. Upon retirement he turned to the cause of Irish Nationalism and the furtherance of Home Rule. Casement's other objective in Germany was to raise a regiment from the Irish prisoners of war to return to Ireland to fight in the Easter Rising, but in this he failed.

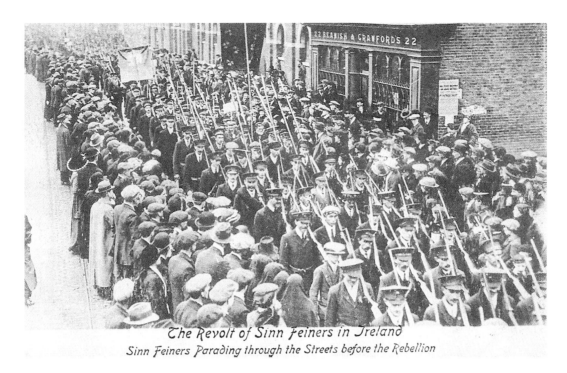

The Revolt of Sinn Feiners in Ireland
Sinn Feiners Parading through the Streets before the Rebellion

This postcard shows a parade of Volunteers, many of them bearing only a pike. Only those at the front of the parade seem to have rifles. This parade, I believe took place at the junction of Georges Street (now Washington Street) and Little Hanover Street in Cork at the end of November 1915.

However, Casement was successful in eliciting a promise of a shipment of arms from the German Government to arrive in time for the Rising. The promised arms were loaded on the *Libau*, a captured Allied vessel formerly known as the *Castro* and now disguised as a Norwegian ship the *Aud*. On Thursday 9th April 1916 the *Aud*, commanded by Lieutenant Spindler, was piloted out of Lubeck Harbour in Germany heading for its destination, Tralee Bay, Ireland.

Due to intercepted coded German naval messages the Admiralty in London were aware of the ship's intentions and informed the officer in command at Queenstown (now Cobh) who set plans in action to intercept the vessel before it could unload its deadly cargo. Spindler arrived in Tralee Bay on Maundy Thursday, 20th April, where he weighed anchor at a prearranged point to rendezvous with the German submarine U-19 that was carrying Casement and his companions back to Ireland. Spindler, realising that staying on station would look more than suspicious, sailed about the bay until dusk to avert any interest from British naval vessels. When dusk fell he signalled constantly to the shore throughout the evening without response, giving up in the early hours of the morning. The following day, Good Friday, 21st April, Spindler managed to evade two British naval ships. Fearing capture and disclosure of his cargo, which his manifest stated as being kitchen utensils, he set a course for the open sea in an effort to put distance between him and the coastal waters commanded by the British Navy. He managed to hoodwink one British naval vessel, claiming a broken engine, but later that afternoon the *Aud* was challenged by H.M.S. *Bluebell*. Spindler tried to bluff his way again, pretending not to understand the orders from the *Bluebell*'s captain. Finally, a warning shot was fired over Spinder's bow, a message he understood totally and at the *Bluebell*'s command he set a course for Queenstown as ordered under escort. The following morning as the vessels approached Queenstown, the *Aud* stopped. It lowered its boats which were quickly filled with scurrying crew members. Then came an explosion. Spindler had scuttled his ship, leaving the Volunteers devoid of arms and sealing the fate of the Rising before it had even started.

At dawn on Good Friday, having failed to make the agreed rendezvous with the *Aud*, Casement, Robert Monteith (a former British soldier and now a member of the I.R.B.) and Private Daniel Bailey left their German U-boat. Adrift in a collapsible boat they made for the shore through choppy waters, landing at Curaghane on Banna Strand. Private Bailey was a member of the Irish Brigade who had only volunteered to go with Casement to free himself from the German prisoner of war camp.

Queenstown Harbour with St. Patrick's Cathedral.

Casement, who had served abroad in several tropical postings, was in poor health and the boat trip had not helped matters. After covering up their boat in the sand dunes the three set out to find their missing contacts. On reaching an Irish ruin known as McKenna's Fort, Casement stopped to rest whilst the other two made for Tralee to contact the local Volunteers. By now the collapsible boat, together with some small arms, had been discovered by a local farmer who informed the Royal Irish Constabulary (R.I.C.). A search party was set up, Casement was discovered at the fort and arrested. After questioning by a Constable Riley, Casement was taken to Ardfest and from there to the police barracks at Tralee. Eventually Monteith and Bailey managed to contact the local Volunteers Commandant, Austin Stack, who set out to look for Casement. On hearing of his arrest Stack tried to intervene and was also arrested but later released. When the true identity of the arrested man was discovered Casement was sent to Dublin and then on to London where he was tried for treason in one of the most high profile cases of the time.

The British Government by now had two of the three men who came from Germany in custody. Casement was in the Tower of London and Bailey had turned King's evidence. Casement was eventually found guilty, his trial tainted by the evidence of his *Black Diaries* that pointed to his homosexual tendencies. He was hanged in Pentonville Prison, London on 3rd August 1916. His body was repatriated to Ireland in 1965 when in bad weather an ageing and ailing President De Valera attended his state funeral before his remains were interred at Glasnevin.

Monteith, despite the efforts of the British Government who sought the help of the *Daily Mirror* by reproducing a postcard of him, managed to evade arrest.

These incidents in the west of Ireland were a serious blow to the physical outcome of the Rising which was now devoid of the great support that the German arms would have made to the Volunteers throughout the country.

By now, plans for the Rising had been in place for several months. Ostensibly the plan was the work of the Volunteers but in truth it was the scheme of the secretive military council of the I.R.B. MacNeill had been totally excluded from these plans and when on Maundy Thursday, 20th April, he became aware of them he angrily confronted Pearse and MacDermott. Embarrassed by their situation the two I.R.B. men placated him by informing him of the shipment due

This postcard shows Casement poring over a real book as opposed to the artistically contrived items on the desktop. The name and date appears to be handwriting, but is printed on the card.

The landing of Roger Casement and Captain Monteith on the coast of Kerry. This postcard shows a fanciful version of the truth and is a posed shot with the faces of the men superimposed.

to be delivered by the *Aud*, so that the whole of the country would take up arms and victory would be assured. MacNeill, satisfied, agreed that Pearse's plans for "manoeuvres" on Easter Sunday were safe and could go ahead.

The real power in Ireland lay in the hands of Sir Matthew Nathan, the Under Secretary for Ireland who ran the day to day business of the country. From his appointment in 1914, and much to the annoyance of Lord Wimborne, Sir Matthew Nathan had taken a laid back attitude to the Nationalists and their "fanciful ideas". As the tension rose coming up to the Easter weekend, Wimborne strongly urged the Under Secretary to issue orders for the arrest of the "Sinn Feiners", but this didn't happen. Despite all the omens the authorities took no preemptive action against the leaders of the forthcoming Rising, Revolution or Rebellion with consequences that are now history.

By Holy Saturday, 22nd April, news had reached Dublin of the two disasters that had befallen the planned Rising, the arrest of Casement and the scuttling of the *Aud*. Undaunted, the I.R.B. leaders were determined to continue with their plans. MacNeill took the opposite view. He had been hoodwinked and then placated earlier that with the arrival of the German arms this would achieve a national uprising. With these arms now at the bottom of Queenstown Harbour there could be no national uprising. His conscience would not allow him to put his name to a plan that would see the Volunteers, of whom he was Commander in Chief, go into battle unarmed and become cannon fodder. By early evening he knew he had to take action to avoid this happening.

Together with The O'Rahilly he drove to St. Enda's, Pearse's school, to confront him. MacNeill was incandescent that once again the I.R.B. had taken action without consulting him and used his reputation as a means to achieve their aims. He told Pearse that he would do everything in his power to stop the Rising taking place. Pearse replied that having used his name he was no longer of any use. Still angry, MacNeill took the action he promised and wrote a countermanding order for the Easter Sunday mobilisation. Finally, MacNeill cycled to the offices of the *Sunday Independent* and placed the following notice: "*Owing to the very critical position, all orders given to the Irish Volunteers for tomorrow, Easter Sunday, are hereby rescinded and no parades, marches, or other movement of Irish Volunteers will take place. Each individual Volunteer will obey this order strictly in every particular*". This he gave to The O'Rahilly who travelled the length and breadth of the country delivering it to I.V. commandants.

MacNeill could do no more but hope that the Volunteers carried out his orders as displayed in the newspaper notice and the countermanding order that he had sent via The O'Rahilly. For this action he would be roundly criticised by many Volunteers, but de Valera insisted that he be respected as the Commander in Chief when both were imprisoned after the Rising.

Easter Sunday was a lonely time for the Irish revolutionaries. In Liberty Hall, the headquarters of Connolly's Irish Transport and General Workers Union, the leaders gathered to discuss at length the predicament they now found themselves in. True revolutionaries are never daunted by the odds and despite the blows the movement had suffered over the previous 72 hours the unanimous agreement was that to free Ireland of the English yoke the only option available was boldness. The Easter Rising would take place, but a day late!

Easter Monday, 24th April, was a bright spring Bank Holiday. Many Dubliners took themselves to the coast or, like many of the British soldiers stationed in Dublin, to the races at Fairyhouse. The deliberations of the Rising's leaders holed up in Liberty Hall the day before were now about to be put to the test.

All the rumours and reports meant that the full Volunteer force did not turn out. Together with the Citizen Army the Volunteers could only muster approximately 1,800 men which meant that some strategic positions could not be occupied.

Just before noon an assorted military column left Liberty Hall, marched down Abbey Street and turned right into Sackville Street (now O'Connell Street). As they reached the G.P.O. Connolly ordered them to "Charge". Soldiers on duty there were taken prisoner and locked up. Confused customers were hurried out of the building. Pearse, flanked by the other leaders, stepped beneath the Doric columned portico of the building, which had recently been renovated at great expense, and read out to bemused passing Dublin citizens the Proclamation of the Irish Republic. The meagre ceremony completed, all returned to the building which was now being turned into a fortress for the ensuing conflict, as windows were smashed and then barricaded. From the roof two flags were flown: at the Prince's Street corner the new green flag bearing in gold lettering the words "Irish Republic" and at the Henry Street corner the green, white and orange tricolour raised by Gearoid O'Sullivan that was to be the National Flag of Ireland.

The "Irish Republic" flag was eventually taken as a prize of war when British troops entered the G.P.O. and was held in the Imperial War Museum, London until 1966, the 50th Anniversary of the Rising, when the flag was repatriated to Ireland and presented to the Toaiseach, Sean Lemass by the Director of the Museum.

POBLACHT NA H EIREANN.
THE PROVISIONAL GOVERNMENT
OF THE
IRISH REPUBLIC
TO THE PEOPLE OF IRELAND.

IRISHMEN AND IRISHWOMEN : In the name of God and of the dead generations from which she receives her old tradition of nationhood, Ireland, through us, summons her children to her flag and strikes for her freedom.

Having organised and trained her manhood through her secret revolutionary organisation, the Irish Republican Brotherhood, and through her open military organisations, the Irish Volunteers and the Irish Citizen Army, having patiently perfected her discipline, having resolutely waited for the right moment to reveal itself, she now seizes that moment, and, supported by her exiled children in America and by gallant allies in Europe, but relying in the first on her own strength, she strikes in full confidence of victory.

We declare the right of the people of Ireland to the ownership of Ireland, and to the unfettered control of Irish destinies, to be sovereign and indefeasible. The long usurpation of that right by a foreign people and government has not extinguished the right, nor can it ever be extinguished except by the destruction of the Irish people. In every generation the Irish people have asserted their right to national freedom and sovereignty; six times during the past three hundred years they have asserted it in arms. Standing on that fundamental right and again asserting it in arms in the face of the world, we hereby proclaim the Irish Republic as a Sovereign Independent State, and we pledge our lives and the lives of our comrades-in-arms to the cause of its freedom, of its welfare, and of its exaltation among the nations.

The Irish Republic is entitled to, and hereby claims, the allegiance of every Irishman and Irishwoman. The Republic guarantees religious and civil liberty, equal rights and equal opportunities to all its citizens, and declares its resolve to pursue the happiness and prosperity of the whole nation and of all its parts, cherishing all the children of the nation equally, and oblivious of the differences carefully fostered by an alien government, which have divided a minority from the majority in the past.

Until our arms have brought the opportune moment for the establishment of a permanent National Government, representative of the whole people of Ireland and elected by the suffrages of all her men and women, the Provisional Government, hereby constituted, will administer the civil and military affairs of the Republic in trust for the people.

We place the cause of the Irish Republic under the protection of the Most High God, Whose blessing we invoke upon our arms, and we pray that no one who serves that cause will dishonour it by cowardice, inhumanity, or rapine. In this supreme hour the Irish nation must, by its valour and discipline and by the readiness of its children to sacrifice themselves for the common good, prove itself worthy of the august destiny to which it is called.

Signed on Behalf of the Provisional Government,
THOMAS J. CLARKE,
SEAN Mac DIARMADA, **THOMAS MacDONAGH,**
P. H. PEARSE, **EAMONN CEANNT,**
JAMES CONNOLLY. **JOSEPH PLUNKETT.**

SINN FEIN REVOLT.
Reproduction of Declaration, April, 1916.

The Proclamation of the Irish Republic (believed to be the work of Pearse) was printed in a small room at Liberty Hall on a second-hand Wharfdale printer, the cost of the paper and printing paid for by the I.T.G.W.U. The document measured 20 inches by 30 inches and was printed on a greyish tinged paper supplied by Saggart Paper Mills, Dublin.

Connolly employed Christopher Brady (a printer) and Michael Molloy and Liam O'Brien (two compositors) who had previously worked for him on his *Workers Republic* newspaper to produce the most important document in Irish history.

For their own safety all three were placed under arrest when they entered Liberty Hall on Easter Sunday so that in the event of a raid by the authorities they could claim immunity. It was planned that the men would print 2,500 copies, although in the end only 1,000 copies were produced. On finding there was a shortage of type the two compositors went to Capel Street to another printer known to them to borrow trays of type which they loaded onto a cart and returned to Liberty Hall. The man who loaned the type was an Englishman, William Henry West. Despite the extra trays of type the men realised there was not enough to complete the Proclamation so they made the decision to print the document in two halves. From the heading down to the end of the third paragraph "among the nations" completed the first half of the printing, whilst the third paragraph beginning "The Irish Republic" to the last two names of the signatories completed the second half of the printing.

All through the document there are "adjustments" to the type. The heading "IRISH REPUBLIC" ends in a C that is suspiciously like an O that has been tampered with. Both "THE PROVISIONAL GOVERNMENT" and "TO THE PEOPLE OF IRELAND" use two different types of O in the lettering due to the shortage of type. The age of the machine and quality of the paper also caused printing problems. The three men toiled through the night and when they had completed the Proclamation it was sent to the G.P.O. There Sean T. O'Kelly was ordered to paste copies around the city. He sent a copy to his mother, which now rests in Leinster House, the Irish Parliament. The copy sent by Thomas Clarke to his wife, Kathleen is now displayed in Kilmainham. On 26th April, when British soldiers entered Liberty Hall, they found the lower half of the Proclamation still set up and promptly printed off copies.

The G.P.O. was now the headquarters of the Rising. Inside, in addition to the "foot soldiers", it was to be home for the next five days to amongst others: Patrick Pearse and his younger brother William (Willie) Pearse, Winifred Carney, James Connolly's secretary and confidant, The O'Rahilly, Desmond Fitzgerald, Sean T. O'Kelly, who later was to become the President of Ireland, Thomas Clarke, Sean MacDermott, James Connolly and Joseph Plunkett. Fighting alongside their "soldiers of destiny" were a group of Cumann na Mban women, the female version of the Volunteers, supporting the G.P.O. garrison in every way possible.

From the Dublin slums came the poor to loot from the exclusive shops items that they desired but had no use for. Soldiers and citizens alike, returning to the city from their day of pleasure, were mystified and shocked to see the happenings, but this was nothing as to what would happen in the city in the coming days. The authorities had been caught on the hop, but already they were putting action plans together. From Athlone artillery was called up, troops were moved from Ulster and from England came reserves, many of whom believed they were being sent to France and the trenches. Central Dublin was now a military zone. The Dublin Metropolitan Police were withdrawn from the streets and only the curious or the foolhardy ventured out to see the proceedings. Peering from around corners or behind some shelter they quickly withdrew at the sound of the bullet's "ping".

In command of the British forces was Brigadier General William Henry Muir Lowe. Lowe had rejoined the army after a long and distinguished career and at the outbreak of the First World War he was given command of the 3rd. Reserve Cavalry Brigade stationed at the Curragh. His plan to defeat the insurgents was a simple one: encircle their positions and then slowly tighten the circle until they surrendered, a plan that eventually proved successful.

The fighting continued during the day at several of the rebel positions. The South Dublin Union was under heavy attack and the Volunteers' task to defend such a large area was nigh on impossible, but it did not stop them from fighting. At St. Stephen's Green the Citizen Army had to retreat into the Royal College of Surgeons building from the trenches they had dug on the Green. The trenches had become death traps as British machine guns placed on the upper floors of the Shelbourne Hotel, which overlooked the Green, made their position untenable.

College of Surgeons, Dublin. It was in this building the garrison of the Citizens Army sought sanctuary at St. Stephens Green.

In Sackville Street the looters were again taking advantage of the situation. Despite several volleys fired over their heads by the Volunteers to break them up the looting continued. Looters, drunk not only on the stolen alcohol but on the success of the previous day, continued, receding only when fired upon and then returning to the sport when things quietened down.

Two horses lie dead in an unknown side street minus their saddlery watched by young boys and men.

In the G.P.O. Patrick Pearse ordered Joseph Stanley, one of the G.P.O. garrison and the owner of the Gaelic Press, to publish *The Irish War News*. Stanley seized O'Keeffe's Printing Works at 3 Halston Street, Dublin to print the world's shortest-lived newspaper. It was printed for one edition only and was a four page quarto size edition packed with false information as to the state of the Rising throughout the country.

In an effort to quell the looting Francis Sheehy Skeffington, together with several clergy from the Pro Cathedral attempted to reason with the crowds but to no avail. In the G.P.O. there were ambivalent feelings about the looters as it was not how the leaders wanted the foundation of the Republic to be, but it was understandable, although how stolen silks and satins would change the life of the poor was hard to fathom.

The first day of the Republic had passed with little action. At the G.P.O., save for the securing of the building and the requisition of commandeered stores, all was quiet. During the day stray Volunteers joined the garrison on hearing that the Rising had started. The building was attacked by a squadron of lancers who were easy targets even for the inexperienced Volunteers. Four of the lancers were shot and several had their horses shot from under them.

In an effort to deter further looting Sheehy Skeffington organised a meeting that evening for like-minded citizens to form a militia to stop such actions. Whilst crossing Portobello Bridge he was arrested and held at the Portobello Barracks. At about midnight Captain John Bowen Colthurst, of the 3rd Irish Rifles, ordered the prisoner to be handed over to him as a hostage. With Sheehy Skeffington in tow he led a raiding party to the Harcourt Road area. Upon leaving the barracks Bowen Colthurst stopped a youth by the name of J.J. Coade and shot him dead. Sheehy Skeffington was left in the charge of a junior officer while Bowen Colthurst and the remainder of the raiding party went on to arrest two editors of loyalist papers, Thomas Dickson of *The Eyeopener* and Patrick J. MacIntyre of *The Searchlight*, then returned with the three arrested men to Portobello Barracks. The next morning, Wednesday 26th April was to bring shame on the British Army and cause an outcry that would go to the very top of the government. Bowen Colthurst ordered a firing party to take the three men out to the barrack yard, stand them against the wall and at his command shoot them. The three were seriously wounded but not dead so he ordered them shot again. In the afternoon of that day Bowen Colthurst led a party of troops searching in Camden Street and caught Volunteer Richard O'Carroll, a Dublin City Councillor. He was taken back to Portobello Barracks and on being asked "Are you a Sinn Feiner?" answered "From the backbone out" whereupon Bowen Colthurst shot him in the lung and had his writhing body dumped in the street. O'Carroll's body was eventually picked up by a bread van and taken to Portobello Hospital where he died ten days later. Bowen Colthurst's murderous actions were not over, however, as later that afternoon in the same area he stopped a teenager who when he failed to give his name was ordered to kneel and was shot in the back of the head.

Bowen Colthurst's actions might never have come to light if it had not been for Major Sir Francis Vane, the commanding officer at the barracks. When his superiors closed ranks over the murders, Vane went direct to Lord Kitchener who ordered Bowen Colthurst to be court martialled. For his action of speaking out Vane was dismissed from the Army. On 6th June Bowen Colthurst was court martialled and found guilty but insane. He was sent to Broadhurst Mental Institution and released after one year. After a long campaign by Mrs. Sheehy Skeffington, Prime Minister Herbert Asquith finally admitted Bowen Colthurst's guilt and he offered her £10,000 compensation. Hanna Sheehy Skeffington refused the money.

The battle for control of Dublin continued unabated. The attack on the Mendicity Institute did not let up. Sean Heuston and his small garrison, tasked with harassing British troop movements for 24 hours, had now held the position for almost 72 hours. In the North King Street area of the city was Linenhall Barracks, the 1770s trade hall for Irish linen. In 1870 it had become an Army barracks and in 1916 it was the Army's pay department. Commandant Edward Daly recognised it as an easy target but it could also be a morale booster for his pressed troops. So a small detachment of Volunteers was sent to attack the barracks, which being lightly defended fell easily and were subsequently set ablaze.

SINN FEIN REVOLT.
Irish War News, April, 1916.

Sinn Fein Revolt, *Irish War News*, April, 1916. This postcard shows the front and back of the ill fated newspaper.

Sinn Fein Revolt, *Irish War News* (pages 2 and 3), April, 1916. The inside pages of the newspaper.

Sinn Feiners on the Roof of their Head-quarters, Liberty Hall, Dublin

These are not "Sinn Feiners" but members of the Citizen Army armed and in uniform ready to protect strikers or for a rising.

Wednesday 26th April was the day of the bloodiest battle of the Rising. Fresh troops from Liverpool had arrived at Kingstown (now Dun Laoghaire) and followed the coastal route into the city via Northumberland Road. The two columns of Sherwood Foresters were raw recruits, most having just completed their basic training; few had fired a gun in combat or in anger, nor faced an enemy or bullets. Most of the men came from many of the villages around Nottingham and knew each other. Many believed they were being sent to the trenches in France. Along their way they came across occasional sporadic fire but nothing was to prepare them or their officers for the hell that they were about to face. In Northumberland Road they were cut to pieces by the men of C Company, 3rd Battalion of the Volunteers. The Volunteers had taken up positions in No. 25, the Parochial Hall and its school and Clanwilliam House, which looked directly over Mount Street Bridge. The Volunteers at No. 25 were Michael Malone, Jimmy Grace, Paddy Byrne and Michael Rowe. At Clanwilliam House were George Reynolds, the brothers Tom and James Walsh, William Ronan, James Doyle, Patrick Doyle, Richard Murphy and Jimmy Grace. Army intelligence had warned of the presence of Volunteers at the school. At the corner of Haddington Road and Northumberland Road in No. 25 the Volunteers poured down a baptism of fire on the virgin soldiers that sent them scurrying for cover that was not there. Bodies soon mounted up with the dead and wounded. Without the grenades and machine guns that were still at the docks the soldiers' task became more deadly as they approached their target. The weight of numbers and the constant attacks eventually enabled them to gain entry to the house at No. 25, killing Grace. Malone escaped only to be captured some days later.

For the soldiers there was more of the same as they approached the school. In Clanwilliam House the Volunteers were firing at any soldier that appeared. The Foresters who were left turned all their attention on Clanwilliam House but with little or no cover were mercilessly slaughtered. With bodies strewn all over the area a brief ceasefire was held as doctors and nurses from Sir Patrick Dun's Hospital collected the wounded and ferried them there.

After the Insurrection.—Linenhall Barracks.

[*Keogh Bros.*

Sinn Fein Rebellion, 1916. Ruins after shelling on Mount St. Bridge Dublin.

This view shows the shell of the building that had been Clanwilliam House. During the battle of Mount Street Bridge several civilians were either killed or wounded helping the Foresters. During the Rising as a whole more Dubliners died than soldiers.

The shrill sound of a whistle signalled the end of the medical amnesty and the resumption of hostilities. The British forces, who now had their grenades, managed to make it to the house and bombed their way through it, room by room, setting it on fire.

Three of the Volunteers in the house were killed but four of them escaped. The official British figures released showed four officers were killed and fourteen wounded with 216 other ranks killed or wounded.

Whilst the insurgents had expected, and received, artillery from the British field guns, a naval bombardment was a surprise. But as "all is fair in love and war" the British enlisted the use of the 12 pounder naval guns of the *Helga* to shell the deserted Liberty Hall building on the Wednesday. There are reports that the only person in the hall was its caretaker, Mr. Peter Ennis who made the hastiest of exits in fear of his life. As with much of the British gunnery many a shell missed its target but found others close by.

Always referred to as the *Helga*, the ship's original name when she was built in 1908 at the Liffey Dockyards for the Department of Agriculture and Technical Instruction was *Helga II*. Soon after the outbreak of the First World War in 1915 she was commandeered by the Admiralty and classified as an armed steam yacht with the title H.M.Y. *Helga*. Her duties were escorting shipping in the Irish Sea and anti-submarine patrols. Later she was credited with the sinking of a German submarine and for rescuing many of the passengers from R.M.S. *Leinster* which was sunk by a German torpedo on 10th October 1918. During the War of Independence she was used as a troop ship for the Black and Tans. In 1923 the ship was handed over to the Irish Free State Navy, becoming one of its first vessels. She was renamed *Muirchu* after the Irish monk and scholar who was known for his study of the life of Saint Patrick. However, the following year she was returned to the department of Agriculture and Fisheries where she remained at her task of fishery protection before becoming part of the Marine and Coastwatching Service until 1947. She was then sold to Hammond Lane Foundry, Dublin. On 8th May 1947, making her way to Dublin, she sunk off the Saltee Islands.

By Thursday 27th April the turning point had been reached with the fulcrum tipping in the balance of the overwhelming British forces. The *Helga* now fired on de Valera's garrison at Ringsend where a water tower had been topped out with a green flag. The naval gunners eventually found their mark and amidst a great shower of water the tower was no more. As amusing a spectacle as this must have appeared it was the population of Dublin and those from the slums in particular who found no fun in their efforts to find food. In the early stages of the Rising shops were looted for the fun of it with luxury items of no intrinsic use to the looters being taken, but with a shortage of the basics more looting took place and food shops were the target.

In Sackville Street the British Army were now in full control and concentrated their efforts on the G.P.O. The rebels' rifle bullets were no match for the artillery shells of their opponents. Inside the building the small improvised first aid station stretched Dr. James (Jim) Ryan, who had yet to qualify, and Dan McLoughlin, a medical student, as they attended to their patients with the sparse medical supplies at their disposal. That afternoon Connolly supervised the placement of his men around Henry Street and was wounded in the arm. After having his wound cleaned and dressed as inconspicuously as possible, he returned to his duties. Moving from the cover of the post office Connolly again risked himself to give orders and by doing so stepped too far into the open. A British bullet ricocheted, smashing into his ankle and leaving him unable to walk. He dragged himself until he reached Princes Street, where he was spotted and taken into the post office. Once inside the building he was taken to the first aid station where Captain John Mahony, a captured British Army doctor, helped attend to him. As the cordon of the British forces was slowly tightening, Edward Daly's Four Courts garrison was coming under increased pressure from the overwhelming numbers of the enemy. In the North King Street area his men were now up against both British guns and armoured vehicles. Unable to make any progress against Daly's garrison the soldiers broke through the walls of the adjoining houses to outflank the insurgents. Many of these houses were still occupied by their owners. Here the men of the South Staffordshire Regiment took it upon themselves to deal with anything or anybody who stood in their way. Men in the houses were shot out of hand as being "Sinn Feiners" and women and children were harshly treated as the soldiers saw fit. Many of these soldiers were men who had recently finished their basic training and had never been in a close encounter conflict before. Many of the insurgents were not in military uniform, wore civilian clothes and fired weapons loaded with 'dum dum' bullets that inflicted dreadful injuries. These bullets were issued in ignorance as to the effect they could cause. To achieve their aim soldiers are liable to take any action needed to save themselves and the lives of their comrades. When the dust of the Rising had settled and events reviewed, the actions of the South Staffs. were justified as actions taken "in the heat of the battle".

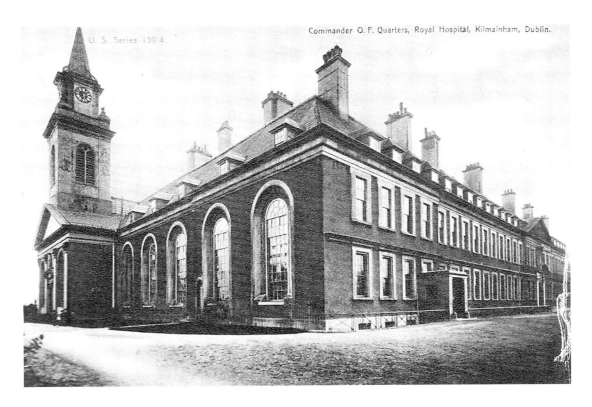

This American postcard shows the magnificent building that was the headquarters of the British Army in Ireland.

Before the sun came up on Friday 28th April General Sir John Maxwell and his staff had sailed up the Liffey and arrived at the North Wall where military vehicles were waiting to take him to the Royal Hospital, Kilmainham, the headquarters of the Commander-in-Chief of the British Forces in Ireland. The scene that greeted him was of areas of utter destruction – buildings reduced to rubble, buildings that revealed themselves as no more than a shell, no roof, floors, windows, or doors, buildings that only existed because of a remaining single standing wall. Dublin resembled a town in the middle of the fighting of the Great War and both rifle and machine gun bullets could be heard whizzing all about. Once in the Royal Hospital Maxwell set about issuing new orders and confirming existing standing orders. The Staffs. were to continue their progress through the Four Courts area and the G.P.O. was now to bear the full weight of the British forces, which were daily being reinforced with fresh regiments from England. Maxwell was going to make his mark even at this late stage of his career, though little did he know it was his later actions that would make his name.

With the dawn came a false lull in the action at the G.P.O., albeit short-lived. The garrison took their breakfast to their posts and hastily reinforced the building's main doors while they waited for the British attack, which was not long in coming. When it did it was not men but mortars that attacked the building. The bombardment of the previous day started up again and, as before, the British artillery had yet to find their range. Consequently the Hotel Metropole took as many direct hits as did the Post Office. As the British shells began to find their target the Post Office was not a happy place. The shells were now making a difference, coupled with bullets from British rifles and machine guns and the floor was in most cases the safest place to be. None the less Pearse and Connolly continued to issue false and optimistic bulletins on the success of the Rising. The Post Office was now totally cut off and it was doubtful if these bulletins ever reached their "target audience".

As bad as the situation was the worst was yet to come when incendiary shells landed on the roof of the building, setting it alight. Men rushed with buckets and hoses, both of which were hopeless against the inferno that was now beginning to take a grip of the roof. With the collapse of the roof fires started on the floors below and the hoses were damaged by the sparks shed by the flames. As the fire took hold floor by floor men evacuated their stations to the floor below. Now it was the Rosary rather than the rifle that men sought for protection.

At St. Stephens Green the Citizen's Army were holding out in all but food, which was now in desperately short supply and taking its toll on the garrison. Men were collapsing from lack of sleep and food not to mention the mental torment of continued attack.

Eamonn Ceannt, Cathal Brugha and Captain Liam Cosgrave continued their fight at the South Dublin Union against all odds. During an agreed ceasefire both sides collected the dead bodies of their comrades from the fighting of the previous night.

At the Jacob's Biscuit Factory the garrison had seen little action and it was to remain so for the rest of the day. De Valera's men at Bolland's Mill were ready for a fight. During the week the garrison had had several skirmishes with British forces. They were keyed up waiting for an attack that never came. De Valera was now suffering from the same tensions as his men, his actions seemingly neurotic, afraid his decisions would imperil his men and their cause.

As the day proceeded it was obvious the G.P.O. and its garrison was in danger not from the British forces and their bullets but from the fire that had now taken a firm hold of the building. By early evening Pearse called together all the women in the building, explained their position and that when the opportunity arose they should leave. Begrudgingly all agreed with the exception of three, Winifred Carney (Connolly's secretary) and two nurses Elizabeth O'Farrell and Julia Grenan who insisted on staying to help with Connolly and the other wounded men. Preparations were made for the women to leave from a door in Henry Street.

With the women safely exited Pearse and Connolly made their plans for the evacuation of their burning headquarters. The wounded from the garrison were slipped out of the building and taken to Jervis Street Hospital. Connolly, who had been given morphine to help his pain, was still in great discomfort and was carried to the Henry Street door in a sheet stretcher. Carried by four Volunteers they dashed across to Henry Place where they rested up in stables owned by the O'Brien Mineral Water Co. It was a miracle that through the hail of bullets anyone could survive but most did manage to eventually make their way to the east side of Moore Street. The bullets did not miss all their targets, one of which was Michael O'Rahilly, The O'Rahilly, who fell and died in a gutter in Moore Street.

Those that did make it to Moore Street tunnelled their way through until they reached No. 16 where the new headquarters were set up. The garrison of almost 200 men had made it from being shot or burnt to death to the safety of Moore Street but only the dawn of the following day would see if their future was secure and that of the five day newly formed Irish Republic.

HOW THE O'RAHILLY FELL. MOOR LANE EASTER !!

This very battered postcard represents the death of The O'Rahilly. It is really a rather badly-drawn cartoon with a facial photograph of him stuck on to the body. The damage to the card has partly obscured the caption which erroneously states MOOR LANE which is spelt wrongly and should in any case be Moore Sreet.

Irish Rebellion. May 1916.
Holding a Dublin street against the Rebels.

This domestic barricade was erected at the junction of Parnell and Moore Street, outside Simpson & Wallace who were butchers at 57 Parnell Street. This barricade may well have been the barricade from which The O'Rahilly and the "Rebels" were shot. The shutters of the shop have been battered and the soldier on the right of the view is resting on the butchers block.

Irish Rebellion. May 1916.
Soldiers holding a Dublin Street.

Irish Rebellion · May 1916.
Guarding one of the Dublin Streets.

Two views of the same makeshift barricade in Talbot Street, taken by the photographer from within enemy territory.

The Sinn Fein Rising.—A type of Armoured Car used during the Revolt.

A Rolls Royce armoured car built on a 40/50 h.p. Silver Ghost chassis fitted with an Admiralty gun turret, pictured at the Royal Barracks, Dublin.

The Insurrection in Dublin.—Armoured Motor Car in Bachelor's Walk.

This "box" on wheels is patrolling Bachelor's Walk after the Rising with the ruined buildings of Hopkins and Hopkins in the background. Over cobbled streets and with solid tyres it must have been an uncomfortable ride. The driver had a restricted view and false gun ports were painted on the side of the vehicle to confuse the insurgents. There was a third vehicle used during the conflict that was constructed at the Inchicore Railway workshop that incorporated an adapted locomotive boiler mounted on a Guinness flat bed lorry.

Chapter 3: Surrender

On the morning of Saturday 29th April the five members of the Provisional Government of the Irish Republic that had exited the G.P.O. and approximately 200 of the G.P.O. garrison were holed up in their new headquarters on the east side of Moore Street at No. 16. Unable to escape the facts, they gathered around Connolly's bed and discussed the possibility of surrender. The decision to do so was made reluctantly. Nurse Elizabeth O'Farrell was asked to mediate, a task that was not without danger. At about 12.30 p.m. she cautiously waved an improvised white flag and walked towards the barricade manned by British soldiers at the end of the street. Here she explained that she had been sent by Pearse to negotiate. She was then taken under escort past Tom Clarke's tobacconist shop in Great Britain Street. Further down the street she was questioned by a British officer who contacted General Lowe to appraise him of the situation. Lowe arrived with his staff officer, Major de Courcy Wheeler. Lowe told the nurse that the only terms he would accept was unconditional surrender and asked her to return to Pearse to convey this.

Surrender Of P,H, Pearse, April, 29, 1916.

This photographic postcard shows Patrick Pearse surrendering to General Lowe. Standing next to General Lowe is a British officer, his son William. Just visible beneath Pearse's coat can be seen another pair of feet, which belong to Nurse Elizabeth O'Farrell.

Returning to Pearse she related Lowe's terms. Pearse then asked her to go back to Lowe and seek protection for his garrison. This she did but was met with the same answer, unconditional surrender or resumption of hostilities. Again she returned to Pearse with the same message: unconditional surrender was the only condition which General Lowe would accept.

Within minutes of returning with Lowe's ultimatum the five members of the Provisional Government held a brief meeting, after which Pearse accompanied by Nurse O'Farrell emerged from No. 16 Moore Street. It was 2.30 p.m. when the two men, Commandant Pearse and General Lowe, met one another at the British barricade at the top of Moore Street, where Pearse handed over his sword together with his automatic pistol, holster and a pouch of ammunition. After this brief ceremony Pearse was driven off in a British staff car accompanied by the General's A.D.C. while the general and Major de Courcy Wheeler went ahead in another car. The convoy took Pearse to Parkgate, Headquarters of the British Irish Command where he was interviewed by General Sir John Maxwell. After writing his surrender document several copies were typed up and he signed them.

In order to prevent the further slaughter of Dublin citizens, and in the hope of saving the lives of our followers now surrounded and hopelessly outnumbered, the members of the Provisional Government present at Head-Quarters have agreed to an unconditional surrender, and the Commandants of the various districts in the City and Country will order their commands to lay down arms.

SINN FEIN REVOLT.
Fac-simile reproduction of Surrender, signed and dated
29th April, 1916.

This postcard shows the document that was signed by four of the Rising's Commandants. What it does not show is the signature of Eamonn Ceannt who signed under the name of Thomas MacDonagh.

That evening Pearse was taken to Arbour Hill Detention Barracks. Overnight it was arranged that Nurse O'Farrell be accommodated in the National Bank in Parnell Street. The following morning, Sunday 30th April, together with Major de Courcy Wheeler, she was driven halfway up Grafton Street. She left the car with only a white flag for protection and amid bullets she made her way to a side door of the Royal College of Surgeons building in York Street. She asked to see Commandant Mallin but was taken to Countess Markievicz as Mallin was catching up on some sleep. The Countess, shocked at the sight of the surrender document, woke her superior and discussed the situation with him. To the annoyance of the major the nurse left the building without getting an agreement of surrender. At about 11.00 a.m., after making arrangements for the hoped-for surrender, de Courcy Wheeler met with Commandant Mallin and Countess Markievicz to agree the surrender of the garrison. The men were to lay down their arms in the building and then form up in ranks outside. After inspecting the abandoned arms in the building the garrison of 109 men and ten women, together with Commandant Mallin and Countess Markievicz, were marched off under heavy guard to Richmond Barracks.

Again, O'Farrell and de Courcy Wheeler were driven to de Valera's garrison at Bolland's Mill. De Valera was unsure as to the action he should take on being presented with the surrender document as many of his men wanted to continue the fight, the garrison had had little combat during the week and were well stocked with supplies. He insisted that he would only surrender after having consulted his superior officer Thomas MacDonagh. At last, at the head of his garrison de Valera led his men marching like a professional army into surrender at Lower Mount Street where they laid down their arms and were marched off to Richmond Barracks.

With the surrender of the G.P.O. garrison Nurse Elizabeth O'Farrell proceeded to the Four Courts garrison of Edward Daly. On her journey she met up with Father Columbus who accompanied her to a side door of the Four Courts. Asking for Commandant Daly they were given further directions and finally came to him with the news of the surrender. At approximately 6 p.m. Daly broke the news to his men, many of who wanted to continue the fight. Eventually, he called his men to order and led them to O'Connell Street and surrendered. Waiting for them there were General Lowe and Major de Courcy Wheeler. The major instructed Daly of the procedure to lay down arms. Daly then ordered his men who performed the task with such dignity and perfection that, to the disgust of General Lowe, Daly and de Courcey Wheeler smartly saluted each other.

Nurse Elizabeth O'Farrell was born in Dublin in 1884 and trained and worked as a midwife at the Holles Street Hospital. A member of Cumann na mban she served in the G.P.O. during the Rising. She was imprisoned for several months despite a plea for clemency by General Lowe for the part she played in the surrender. She remained true to the Republican cause all her life and died on 25th June 1957 at Fatima House, Bray, Co. Wicklow. She is buried alongside Julia Grenan, Connolly's secretary, in the Republican plot at Glasnevin Cemetery.

Chapter 4: Aftermath

After agreeing to the unconditional surrender and presenting his sword to General Lowe, Pearse was taken to Arbour Hill Barracks. Connolly, who could only be stretchered, was taken to a room in Dublin Castle, confined to bed and watched over night and day by a military guard.

According to the conditions of the surrender the men of the G.P.O. garrison were to march up to the line of soldiers at the Gresham Hotel, halt, take five paces forward and lay down their arms, after which they were to be searched and asked for their name and address. They were then taken to the grass patch at the front of the Rotunda, where they were watched over by soldiers with bayonets fixed and a machine gun crew. Unbeknown to them this would be their "accommodation" for the night with no cover or protection from the chill of an early spring night. Later on they would be joined by Edward Daly's Four Courts garrison. During the night an Irish officer by the name of Captain Lee Wilson took over command of the prisoners. It was said that he had been drinking and in a despotic rage began hurling insults and taunts on his captives, after which Clarke, MacDiarmada and Daly were taken away and strip searched. The following day about noon, still stiff, cold and tired the prisoners were marched off to Richmond Barracks. Along the way they were subjected to abusive advice on how the soldiers should "take care" of them. Unlike Pearse and Connolly, Tom Clarke had remained with the main body of the G.P.O. garrison after they laid down their arms. He also marched to Richmond Barracks and was court martialled there on Monday 1st May. That evening the 58 year old spiritual leader of the Rebellion was moved to Kilmainham. After midnight Kathleen, his wife, who had been held in Dublin Castle, was brought over for them to say their good-byes. Thomas J. Clarke was executed in the early hours of Wednesday 3rd May.

After Pearse had surrendered to General Lowe he was taken to Arbour Hill Barracks where he was held until his court martial on Tuesday 2nd May at Richmond Barracks. During this time he wrote many touching letters to family and friends and a statement to General Maxwell. He addressed the court martial, but the result was a foregone conclusion that was expected by all those put on trial. The only concession for the accused was that they would be shot by firing squad, a death reserved for soldiers, as opposed to hanging, the penalty usually meted out to common criminals. He also was executed on Wednesday 3rd May.

At 3 o'clock on the afternoon of Sunday 30th April MacDonagh met with General Lowe and surrendered after consulting with Eamonn Ceannt. After arranging the surrender details with his men MacDonagh was taken to Richmond Barracks where on the morning of Tuesday 2nd May he was tried by court martial. That evening in his cell at Kilmainham he wrote a statement detailing he knew he was to die at 3.30 a.m. the following day. The statement went on to explain the parlous state of his finances and qualified the sentiment he made at his court martial ending with his love to his wife Muriel, son Donagh and daughter Barbara. That night he was visited by his sister, Sister Francesca, a nun at Basin Lane Convent. He too was executed early the following morning, Wednesday 3rd May.

After their surrender Daly and his men were marched off to the grassy plot in front of the Rotunda Hospital where the other insurgents were being held. The following day all were escorted under armed guard to Richmond Barracks where on Wednesday, 3rd May Daly was court martailled and that evening transferred to Kilmainham. In the early hours of Thursday 4th May he was visited by his sisters, Laura and Madge Daly and Mrs. Kathleen Clarke. Later that morning he was taken to the stone breakers yard and shot.

THE ROTUNDA HOSPITAL, DUBLIN

This *circa* 1930s postcard shows the green in the front of the building where the insurgents were kept overnight.

On Saturday 29th April the remaining garrison of the G.P.O. were led out of their headquarters at 16 Moore Street by William Pearse and Joseph Mary Plunkett waving white flags. With the rest of the garrison they spent the night at the Rotunda Hospital before being marched off the following morning to Richmond Barracks. It is unclear when William Pearse was court martialled, but it was probably on Wednesday 3rd May after which he was sent to Kilmainham, where in the early hours of Thursday 4th May he was visited by his mother and Margaret, his sister, before his execution.

After discussions with MacDonagh at the South Dublin Union, Ceannt accepted the surrender to be the best outcome for his men. The British army commander was astonished when he learned that the area had been held by just 42 Volunteers. Leaving the Union at the head of his garrison Ceannt marched them to the Marrowbone Lane Distillery where both garrisons joined and marched to the corner of Bride Street and Ross Road. There, under the watchful eyes of the British military, the men laid down their arms. Ceannt was taken to Richmond Barracks where at 10 o'clock on Thursday 4th May he was court martialled. Here he wrote to his wife Aine and his young son Ronan telling them of his expected death sentence. It is believed that by Saturday 6th May he was in cell 88 at Kilmainham where he saw his wife on Sunday 7th May before being moved to the ground floor of the prison and placed in cell 20. He wrote his last letter to his wife at 2.30 a.m. on the morning of Monday 8th May. Soon after he walked with Father Augustine to the yard where he was asked to sit on a box with hands tied and eyes blindfolded. With the sound of the rifles, his dead body slumped forward.

On Sunday 30th April MacDermott, whose walking stick had been taken from him, limped to Richmond Barracks under special guard. There he was placed in a large room containing dozens of prisoners and a large vomit retching tank that was used as a latrine. Incandescent with rage he banged on the door until soldiers arrived. He let out a tirade of indignation, so much so that the men were allowed buckets to empty the tank, which was then disinfected. At Richmond Barracks he was held in a room in Block L with other men. On the night of Monday 8th May he was notified by a British officer that he was to be court martialled the following day. On hearing this news he is alleged to have said "Let's have a concert", which by all reports they did. After his trial he was moved to Kilmainham, most likely on the same day, Tuesday 9th May.

Sinn Fein Rebel Leaders under Arrest
" Major" McBride (central figure nearest camera) being
marched off under escort

During the evening of 10th May he was visited by Rev. Dr. Patrick Browne of Maynooth who spent several hours with him. The next day he was informed of the expected verdict of the court martial, that he was to be executed the following day. In the short time he had left he wrote to his brothers and sisters and to John Daly, the ageing Limerick Fenian. At his request he was visited by the sisters Phyllis and Mary Ryan. According to Miss Mary Ryan "We were there at twelve o'clock and we didn't leave until three". All this time they were in MacDermott's cell with a soldier standing in the doorway. The sisters left at 3 o'clock when a priest arrived. By 3.45 a.m on Friday, 12th May Sean MacDermott was no longer alive.

After Pearse had surrendered on 29th April Connolly was carried out from Moore Street by a Volunteer party commanded by Diarmuid Lynch. The party consisted of Seamus Devoy, Joseph Fellon, P.J. Byrne, Michael Staines, Michael Nugent and Liam Tannam. The stretcher party stopped in Great Britain Street (now Parnell Street) outside Tom Clarke's tobacconist shop where Connolly spoke to General Lowe. They then continued via Capel Street, escorted by a detachment of a British officer and sixteen soldiers. On arriving at Dublin Castle Connolly was received by the British Red Cross and placed in a small ward in the officers quarters in the castle. The stretcher party were arrested and marched off to Ship Street Barracks.

STATE DRAWING ROOM, DUBLIN CASTLE RED CROSS HOSPITAL.

Dublin Castle Red Cross Room. This was not the only room used as a ward; the Throne Room was also laid out with beds.

Whilst Connolly was having his wounds dressed in his room Major de Courcy Wheeler, Lowe's staff captain, came to him and asked if he had read Pearse's surrender document and if he would agree to sign it. Connolly said he would dictate his own surrender and the major wrote in his own hand Connolly's terms beneath Pearse's typewritten script. Then Connolly signed and dated it. The following day, Low Sunday, 30th April, Connolly was visited by Fathers Augustine and Aloysius who were taken to his room where he was being watched over by an armed soldier, and talked to him to confirm that the surrender was genuine. On Sunday 7th May Mrs. Connolly received a letter granting her permission to visit her husband on the mornings of the following Monday or Tuesday, the 8th or 9th. Mrs. Connolly, whose nerves were fraught, was mistakenly consoled by the belief that they would never execute a wounded man. On Tuesday 9th May Connolly was tried by court martial and that same day he was again visited by his wife, Lily, and their eldest daughter, Nora. At 11 o'clock on Thursday 11th May Connolly was woken from his sleep to be told of his execution the following day. In the early hours of Friday 12th May Lily and Nora were called to Dublin Castle where Connolly confirmed that he was to be shot later that morning. During an upsetting and tearful parting he smuggled to his daughter a copy of his court martial statement. Connolly was taken to Kilmainham where, propped on a chair, he was shot, the last man of the short-lived Independent Irish Republic signatories to die for his country. His death marked the end of the ill-fated Easter Rising of 1916 in Dublin.

The bodies of the fourteen executed men were taken to Arbour Hill Military Detention Centre where they were put in a mass grave and liberally covered with quicklime. The government wanted no repeat of some nationalist making propaganda speeches as happened over the grave of O'Donovan Rossa when Pearse said "The fools, the fools, the fools, they have left us our Fenian dead and while Ireland holds these graves Ireland unfree shall never be at peace". Today the site is a quiet peaceful setting with the names of the men cut in stone surrounding a simple grass plot. It is a shrine not only for Irish men and women but also for dignitaries who are on state visits to Ireland. Today we may consider the execution of these brave men as harsh and would be very wary of the public's response to such a course of action, something that was less of a consideration in 1916. One hundred years ago life was harsher than today. The most brutal of wars was only halfway through its course, the death penalty existed, deserters at the Front were shot in front of their regiments and conscientious objectors were given white feathers by women and girls.

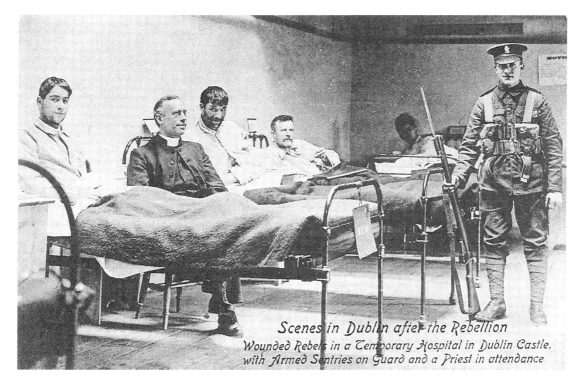

Scenes in Dublin after the Rebellion
Wounded Rebels in a Temporary Hospital in Dublin Castle, with Armed Sentries on Guard and a Priest in attendance

This facility, though not in such salubrious surroundings was also afforded to those insurgents wounded during the Rising but with "nurses" with fixed bayonets rather than bedpans. Despite the presence of the soldier all the Rebels seem relaxed.

After the first of the executions constant representations were made to both General Maxwell and Prime Minister Asquith to halt them. Asquith wrote to Maxwell on the matter without fully ordering him to stop them. Questions were asked in Parliament and M.Ps from both sides strongly questioned the Government's actions. Noted personalities wrote and made speeches calling for a stop to the executions, amongst them George Bernard Shaw, the Irish author. Editorials in the press, whilst holding the government line, were sympathetic to the plight of the condemned, though always careful of not crossing the line of public opinion held in England.

Dublin, where the Rising was at its strongest, was not a happy place. The centre of Dublin was a ruin, much of the city's infrastructure had been destroyed and half or more of Sackville Street had been blown away. The cost of the devastation to the city was estimated to be in the region of £2,750,000, a not inconsiderable amount. There had been and still were food shortages as goods shipped across the Irish Sea from England and further afield dried up. The postal system was in disarray so that letters to and from soldiers fighting in the war were at best delayed and many were lost in the charred ruins of the G.P.O. In Dublin in particular there was anger against the Rising and those who participated in it. The wives of men fighting in the British Army who depended on their husbands' pay were fearful that their money would not be paid. In the countryside farmers were getting rich growing the food and rearing the livestock needed to feed an ever-expanding army, and wanted nothing to disrupt their income. Provisions of all sorts were in short supply and movement around the city difficult. Although Dubliners were upset and angry with the insurgents, the executions exacerbated their anger towards the British Government. Angry they were at the Rising, indignant they were at the execution of Irishmen. Overnight throughout the country these men, this Rising, became intrinsically linked to not only Irishness but to hatred for the English and highlighted the cause for which they had fought and died. Simple little pieces of cardboard with the portraits of the fallen took on the sacredness of Russian icons. Next to the holy pictures of the Sacred Heart and the Virgin Mary were placed these postcards of modern day martyrs on windowsills and mantelpieces throughout the land and in front of them votive candles offered for saving of their souls.

Apart from the executed men it is estimated that another 3,500 people across the country were arrested though most arrests were in and around the Dublin area. Many of those who took part in the Rising were "Sentenced to Death; Sentence Commuted to Penal Servitude for Life". No one served a life term. Others were sentenced to ten or 20 years "Penal Servitude" to be served in a variety of English prisons, amongst them Lewes Prison in Sussex.

Sinn Fein Rebellion, Dublin
A Rebel Prisoner being
marched over O'Connell Bridge

Not all of the insurgents laid down their arms at the time of the surrender and occasionally a straggler would be found and brought into custody. The "Rebel Prisoner" is believed to be James O'Connor who managed to escape when the Ashborne garrison surrendered.

Life in Dublin was still being disrupted. Everywhere in the centre of the city and the Sackville Street area in particular there were piles of rubble with the stench of burnt-out fires hanging in the air, but there was to be more destruction and disruption to come. Many buildings were less than a shell and some only remained with one wall upright. They were a danger to the citizens and in some cases to those who would be tasked with their destruction.

With the executions over, the Prime Minister, Herbert Asquith, felt it was safe for him to do his duty by coming to Dublin to see for himself the havoc that the Rising had caused. On Friday 13th May he came and was given a guided tour of the destroyed city, the detention centres and how the city was returning to some form of normality. On Sunday 15th May he attended a parade in College Park and a march past by the Dublin Volunteer Training Corps. On a makeshift platform, constructed with two park benches and wooden planks, he took the salute together with other prominent dignitaries.

Though the city was slowly getting back to normal the authorities were ever mindful of their slackness in the days leading up to the Rising. Therefore at strategic points around the city small groups of soldiers were stationed not only to reassure citizens that normality had been restored but to deter any troublemakers that this time the army was ready. With rumours still abroad, the majority of which bore no credence, a policy of stop and search was imposed with no one exempt from the policy.

The Review of the Dublin Volunteer Training Corps in the College Park, by General Sir John Grenfell Maxwell.—The picture, reading from left, shows General Sir John Maxwell, Lady Wimborne, Mr. H. H. Asquith, Miss Grosvenor, Mr. Bonham

The picture from left shows General Sir John Maxwell, Lady Wimborne, Mr. H.H. Asquith, Miss Grosvenor, Mr. Bonham Carter (Asquith's private secretary) and General Friend. With the exception of General Friend all seem to be putting on a brave face.

Ruins of Sackville Street, Dublin (Earl Street Corner).

A ruined building that had to be demolished for safety's sake.

After the Insurrection.—Ruins of Eden Quay

Crowds gather for the demolition of a dangerous building at No. 5 Eden Quay. For crowd control Dublin Metropolitan Police stand by and to be extra sure the army has sent a Rolls Royce armoured car.

After the Insurrection.—Ruins in Eden Quay. The fall of a dangerous building.

The fall of a dangerous building. The same Dubliners who came for the fireworks are rewarded as the wall of the building comes crashing down through the dust. The apexed building on the right of the view was an electricity substation that was demolished in 1966 to be replaced by a bus shelter.

Irish Rebellion, May, 1916.

Soldiers bivouacking opposite Liberty Hall,
the Rebel Headquarters in Dublin.

Smoke rises from the camp fire to engulf the Butt Line Bridge above the soldiers.

Sinn Fein Rebellion, Dublin
Priests asked to produce their Papers

The two priests, Dr. Hickey (left) and Monsignor Walsh (right), have been stopped across the
road from the premises of James H. Webb who were tailors and clothiers at 56 Henry Street.

Irish Rebellion, May, 1916.
Searching a hay-cart for Rebels or Ammunition.

This British officer satisfies himself that there is nothing untowards with this load of hay while the cart driver looks laconically on.

It took time to court martial all those who were arrested so prisoners were allowed visitors before being sent to English and Scottish prisons. The insurgents were subsequently held in Lewes Prison, Sussex; Knutsford Prison, Cheshire; Wakefield Prison, West Yorkshire; Wandsworth Prison, London; Stafford Prison, Staffordshire and prisons in Glasgow and Perth. The largest community of insurgents were placed at Wakefield, which held 749. Knutsford held 624; the first of these men arrived on 1st May and the last group on 16th June. Stafford received 550 prisoners whilst Wandsworth took 298 men and the last of the English prisons used was Lewes which took in a mere 59 insurgents arriving at the prison on 20th May. The two Scottish prisons between them held 197 men. Richmond Barracks confined 211 men. There were many hundreds more who were released as the case against them was not found and a few where there was a case of mistaken identity. Ultimately the majority of prisoners were released by Christmas 1916. These figures are approximate numbers.

This view depicts Mr. and Mrs. Cotter visiting their sons, probably at Richmond Barracks. The Cotters lived at 32 St. Ann's Road, Drumcondra and had three sons – Joseph, Richard and Thomas – who all took part in the Rising.

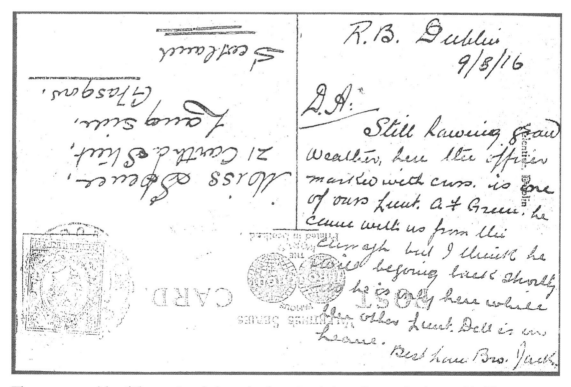

The message side of the postcard above is almost as interesting as the front of it. The message reads: "Still having grand weather here, the officer marked with a cross is one of ours Lieut. A.F. Green is on leave." Lieutenant Green was commissioned as a temporary 2nd Lieutenant in the Army Service Corps on 12th July 1915. On 11th March 1916 he was promoted to acting Captain, a rank he held until the end of the war.

Sinn Fein Rebellion, Dublin   Friends Visiting Sinn Fein Prisoners

This photograph seems to have been taken from inside the prisoners' compound or by poking a camera through the barbed wire enclosing them. It would also appear that the prisoner in the middle of this view is being given an apple or some other piece of fruit. Soldiers with fixed bayonets attend proceedings.

The County Jail, Lewes.

The County Jail, Lewes. This 1906 postcard of the jail looks idyllic, a nice place for a "stretch". The prison was built for adult males in 1853. In 1916 its illustrious prisoners included de Valera, Thomas Ashe, Harry Bolland and Frank Lawless.

Courthouse and Prison, Knutsford

Courthouse and Prison, Knutsford. Built in 1818 to a design by George Moneypenny the prison was extended in 1846 and 1867. It was closed in 1914 as a prison and a year later became an Army Detention Centre. At the end of the First World War it was taken over by the Church of England before being demolished in 1934.

Frongoch was the site of a former Welsh whisky distillery that was being used as a German prisoner of war camp during the First World War. Frongoch's small station on the Bala to Blaenau Festiniog line was mainly used to serve the distillery. The site consisted of two camps, the North Camp and the South Camp, both of which were hot in the summer and cold in the winter.

Concentration Camp, Frongoch, Bala.

The creation of Frongoch Camp, 'the university of the revolution', was arguably the biggest mistake the British Government made after the Easter Rising. This view shows the tall chimney of the distillery and was probably taken from the North Camp.

Those taken prisoner after the Easter Rising were incarcerated in British prisons throughout the land. To relieve these overcrowded prisons the German prisoners of war were moved out of Frongoch and replaced by the insurgents from the Easter Rising. The thinking behind this move was that, apart from relieving the British prisons, having all the Irish prisoners "under one roof" would enable the authorities to keep a better eye on them. This was a big mistake.

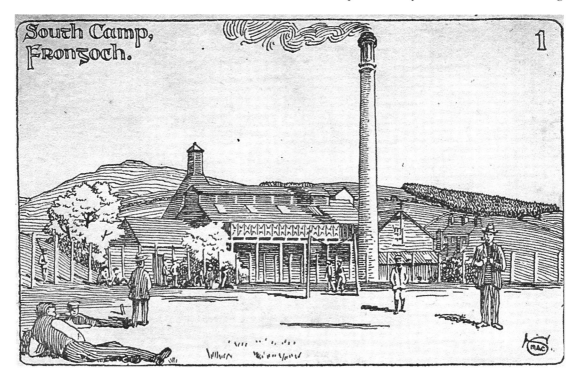

South Camp, Frongoch. This postcard depicts the very leisurely state that the prisoners were held in, but on the far left a sentry is keeping an eye on proceedings.

Another drawing, this time of the North Camp, which was situated on ground above the South Camp, though life again seems very leisurely.

The prisoners were housed in wooden huts that held the "cream" of Irish revolutionaries. In these huts the men of the I.R.A. bonded. Michael Collins made his mark and became not only the camp leader but the future leader of his country. Here the interned men learnt the Irish language, rekindled their Irishness and learnt revolutionary skills.

On 9th June 1916 the gates of Frongoch were opened to receive 2,519 prisoners, but by 29th July 650 had been released and returned to Ireland. Those that remained were bonded into a camaraderie that was to last until the birth of their nation and beyond and in some cases be their downfall. Here the plans were made for the continuation of the struggle for independence and in the "University of Revolution" were fostered the elite that were to rule Ireland over the next 50 years.

On 21st December 1916 the Secretary of State for Ireland, Henry Duke, announced in the House of Commons that all the prisoners held in Frongoch were to be released unconditionally. For once the saying "I'll be home for Christmas" rang true and the prisoners were released on 23rd December 1916.

The Rising, like most other conflicts, generated a collection of memorabilia like the half-printed Proclamations which fetch huge prices at auctions due to their scarcity, but the most important and famous item to come out of this conflict must surely be the green 'Irish Republic' flag. Taken as a prize of war the green poplin flag has the words Irish Republic painted in gold with white highlighting. At the Henry Street corner of the G.P.O. building the Irish tricolour of green, white and gold was raised by Gearoid O'Sullivan, a member of the garrison from Cork. Due to the thinness of the material the painted words from the other side of the flag can be seen. The flag was taken to England and held in the Imperial War Museum, London until 1966. That year, the 50th anniversary of the Rising, the flag was presented to the Taoiseach, Sean Le Mass by the director of the London museum and it is now on display in the National Museum, Collins Barracks, Dublin.

Irish Rebellion - May 1916.
A group of Officers with the captured rebel flag.

This group of British officers are gathered at the base of the Parnell Monument. It appears that the flag is mounted on some form of stick which is at the end of the rifle where the bayonet is attached. It should be noted that the flag is displayed upside down. This is not a mistake, but a common form of insult to the captured standard to indicate defeat.

Parnell's Monument, Dublin.

The monument in honour of Charles Stewart Parnell is sited at the north end of Sackville Street and drew huge crowds at its unveiling on 1st October 1911. It was designed by Augustus Saint Gaudensan, a Dublin-born American who died before it was completed. The monument is 57ft tall and carries an 8ft bronze statue which stands on a 9ft plinth. The obelisk is of granite.

This postcard has the distinction of having the longest caption of all Easter Rising postcards, but makes no mention of the revolvers or the water bottle.

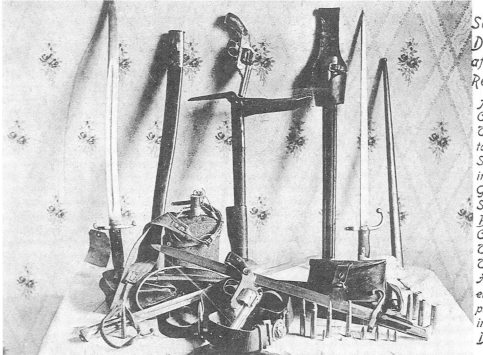

Scenes in Dublin after the Rebellion

A Doctor's Collection of Trophies taken from Sinn Feiners, including German Swords, Belts, Cartridges, Trenching Tools, Haversacks, etc., photographed in Dublin Castle

Chapter 5: Elsewhere

Whilst Dublin was the focal point of the Easter Rising there were four other locations of the conflict. Ashbourne, Co. Meath is some 12.5 miles from Dublin and is a verdant area of fields and hedgerows. As the fight in Dublin was coming to a close this quiet part of the country found itself at the centre of a bloody battle that was to be a tactical template of future battles during the War of Independence.

On Sunday 23rd April the men of the 5th Fingal Battalion of the Irish Volunteers, numbering over one hundred, paraded together with their commanding officer Commandant Thomas Ashe, the company adjutant Dr. Richard Hayes and the quartermaster Frank Lawless.

They were marched to Saucertown for military manoeuvres. Ashe sent Joseph Lawless, the son of Frank, to Dublin to contact James Connolly for operational orders. Joseph returned late that same day with the message that the battalion should stay in readiness. Confused by this order, that evening Hayes and Frank Lawless drove to Dublin for clarification of the orders. Returning in the early hours of the morning the officers decided to stand down the battalion. Early the following morning, Easter Monday, Frank Lawless was woken from his bed by a despatch rider with an order from P.H. Pearse to "Strike at one o'clock today". Joseph was sent off to the home of Hayes where Ashe and Richard Coleman were staying overnight. On Ashe's command Joseph was again sent off to alert the four company commanders to mobilise at Knocksedan, two miles from Swords.

Many of the battalion failed to turn out, suspecting that it was a false alarm as the previous day; consequently the battalion was only at half strength. Ashe sent a section of his men to dynamite the railway bridge at Rogerstown in an effort to stop British reinforcements reaching Dublin. The explosion was loud and the track badly damaged but the bridge held firm. Returning to their camp at Finglas the men cut telegraph wires. Further orders were received from Dublin to hold the main Finglas road and take prisoners of any returning officers from the Fairyhouse Races, although by the evening none had been captured. Later that evening Ashe detailed a company of his Volunteers under Captain Richard Coleman to attack the railway station at Blanchardstown. Unfamiliar with the area the company got lost and aborted their mission and returned to their camp. The following morning, Tuesday 25th April, Ashe received an order from Connolly to send a section of his men to fight in Dublin which he did under the command of Coleman. The loss of these men was helped by the arrival of Lieutenant Richard Mulcahy and two other Volunteers and later in the day by another group who had been cut off from the 1st Battalion and had made their way to Ashe's camp at Knocksedan. Mulcahy was made second in command of the battalion, and that evening Ashe and his officers laid plans for the following day's actions, the attack on the police barracks at Swords and Donabate.

Early the following morning the Volunteers cycled to Swords in three groups. The constables at the barracks were taken by surprise and thought the Volunteers were "playing soldiers"; they were not and the barracks were easily taken. Whilst the constables were held under armed guard the barracks were stripped of arms and ammunition. In the village the Volunteers cut telegraph wires and commandeered food stocks and a bread van that was making a delivery.

On the outskirts of Donabate a shot was fired, alerting the police barracks. The barracks were surrounded and offered terms of surrender which was met by a volley of bullets. The Volunteers' bullets had little effect on the building so the decision was taken for the Volunteers to literally smash their way in. With the front door taken out the constables realised their plight and surrendered. As at Swords the barracks was swept for arms and ammunition, the constables were warned not to return and released. Before leaving the town the railway track and points were destroyed and food purchased from a local store. That evening Ashe and his officers met to plan the attack on Garristown Barracks and Post Office the following day.

In the early hours of Thursday 27th April the battalion left their camp and cycled to the target. Arriving as on previous days three columns came into the town and surrounded the barracks. A garrison of one constable was manning the barracks and he surrendered, allowing the Volunteers to search the building that was devoid of any arms. All the other constables had judiciously moved to the barracks at Balbriggan. All that was taken from Garristown was money from the post office and for that a receipt was given. Returning from the day's action the camp moved later to Borranstown and billeted themselves in an old farm building. Later that night a planning meeting was held for the attack on the Midland Great Western Railway at Batterstown. After breakfasting on Friday 28th April Ashe's Volunteers moved off in three columns, but before reaching the railway had to pass the Ashbourne barracks. The barracks had only recently been reinforced with extra constables and ammunition. Approaching Ashbourne the lead section of the Volunteers captured three R.I.C. constables, one of whom managed to escape. The other two sections had by now surrounded the barracks. Ashe called on the barracks to surrender but his offer was met with volleys of rifle bullets from inside. A gun battle ensued which damaged the building but did not threaten its existence.

Mulchay took cover behind hedges and set up covering fire while Peader Blanchfield fused a bomb which he lobbed at the front of the barracks. The bomb had the desired effect and a white flag was soon seen protruding from the building, followed by the surrendering constables. As they emerged a shot rang out and while the Volunteers' attention was momentarily diverted the constables rushed back into the barracks. The shot had come from the lead car of a fleet of assorted motor vehicles that had been commandeered, some with their drivers, that contained armed constables. The Volunteers turned their attention and fire power on these vehicles which were now stopped in their tracks. Making use of the hedges and ditches that lined the road the Volunteers were able to move unseen into killing positions.

The Volunteers were now positioned on both sides of the road. As the constables stepped out of the vehicles to mount an attack they came under deadly fusillades from the rifles and guns of the Volunteers. Men and vehicles were shattered, bodies and broken glass covered the road, leaving dead, dying and wounded where they fell. The only safety was in the ditches at the roadside, which soon filled with the bodies alive and wounded of the R.I.C. The constables tried to shoot back at the Volunteers but any movement brought a rain of bullets on them. Cover could be found under the vehicles but movement brought the same response. They were sitting targets for the guns of the Volunteers.

The barracks were now covered front and rear. Behind the lines a medical unit was set up in an old cottage by Dr. Hayes. Mulcahy moved a section of his men to the rear of the motor column. During this fierce fight Volunteer Thomas Rafferty was badly injured in the head and had to be taken to Dr. Hayes. Police and Volunteers were firing at each other from point blank range. Mulcahy ordered his men to fix bayonets and charge the hapless constables in the ditches. Many of the constables surrendered but some managed to find safety in farm buildings nearby. Seeing the effects of the charge Frank Lawless ordered his section to do likewise. Led by Inspector Smyth the constables started to make a fight of it until Lawless' gun sent him sprawling, dead before he hit the ground. The other constables immediately surrendered. During this fight Volunteer John Crenigan was killed. The battle was over but had raged close on six hours. The barracks now capitulated, giving up fifteen constables and an officer. Permission was granted for the body of the dead Inspector Smyth to be taken to his home. Wounded constables were helped to the medical unit set up by Dr. Hayes who treated friend and foe alike. Those he was unable to treat were sent in one of the police vehicles to the hospital in Navan. A horse and cart owned by John Austin was used to collect the dead bodies of the police and take them to the washhouse at the barracks. The Volunteers had lost one man killed and six wounded, Thomas Rafferty so badly he could not be moved. Those constables who survived the battle were cautioned not to take up arms again against the Irish Republic and released. The discarded weapons of the R.I.C were collected and were an added burden as the Volunteers left the scene of the battle to camp near Kilsallaghan.

On the morning of Saturday 29th April news reached them of the death of Thomas Rafferty. The remainder of the day was spent overhauling the cache of weapons they had acquired and relaxing from the tough week they had had. To enable this, sentries were placed beyond the perimeter of the camp. The following morning, Sunday 30th April, at about 11 o'clock two R.I.C. officers travelling in a motor car bearing a white flag were stopped on the outskirts of the camp. They were questioned and asked to see the commanding officer. Taken before Ashe and his officers, the two men presented a copy of Pearse's surrender document. Unsure of the validity of the document Ashe agreed to hold one of the officers hostage whilst Mulcahy went to Dublin for verification. He was taken to Arbour Hill where he met with Pearse in his cell. Ninety minutes later Mulcahy returned to the camp confirming their worst fears. The mood in the camp was to continue fighting, but eventually sense prevailed and the 5th Fingal Brigade of the Irish Republic marched to Swords where British army lorries were waiting to transport them into captivity at Richmond Barracks.

On Tuesday 2nd May, without being tried, many of the men were loaded into cattle boats and sent to English prisons. Mulcahy was sent to Knutsford and then to Frongoch detention camp in North Wales. Frank Lawless was sent to Lewes and Thomas Ashe was sent to Dartmoor.

Back in 1915 Paul Galligan had been sent by Dublin to sort out an internal squabble that had arisen in the Wexford Volunteers' ranks. Though Seamus Doyle and Seamus Rafter were in command of the company Galligan's Dublin connections meant unofficially he "called the shots". As the Rising approached confusing orders emanated from Dublin. Late on the night of Saturday 22nd April Galligan took it upon himself to travel to Dublin to clarify the situation and obtain orders for the Volunteers.

Early on Easter Sunday morning, 23rd April, Galligan read MacNeill's countermanding order that cancelled "parades and marches … of Irish Volunteers". The following day, Easter Monday, hearing of the events in the city centre he made his way to the G.P.O. where he met with Pearse and Connolly. He now had orders to attack the railway line from Wexford to stop British troop reinforcements getting to Dublin from the ports of New Ross and Waterford, and not to bother with attacking police barracks as this would be wasteful of ammunition.

Galligan was supplied with a bicycle and set off back to Enniscorthy in the early hours of Tuesday 25th April, eventually arriving late in the evening of Wednesday 26th April. The following morning, 200 Volunteers took control of the town of Enniscorthy. They seized the castle, surrounded the police barracks and cut off its utilities and took over the Athenaeum Town Hall as their headquarters, above which now flew the tricolour of the Irish Republic. Volunteer patrols were set up to police the town and the public houses were closed down. Shots were exchanged with the police in Rafter Street. One constable received a leg wound and was allowed to go to the hospital. The railway station was attacked and taken over, the line was destroyed and several police barracks were left deserted as the Volunteers advanced and took the town of Ferns.

On Saturday 29th April the Volunteers' numbers had grown to 1,000 men as smaller companies from the surrounding areas joined the Enniscorthy garrison. During the morning news reached them that British forces were being gathered to attack the town. Galligan mobilised his men to set up road blocks, trees and telegraph poles were felled, outposts were set up to hinder any advancing troops.

The British reinforcements were under the command of Lieutenant-Colonel French, a retired British army officer who lived locally. At his disposal were 1,000 men and several field guns. During most of Sunday 30th April there was no sighting of the impending British force. However, an R.I.C. inspector and sergeant under the cover of a white flag of truce did appear with a copy of Pearse's surrender document. Alert to the possibility of a trick the two policemen were placed under armed guard. It was decided that a request should be made to Colonel French for Seamus Doyle and Sean Etchingham to be allowed to go to Dublin to speak with Pearse in person. A military car was provided that took the two men to Pearse in Arbour Hill where he confirmed the document to be genuine and signed another copy that was brought back to Enniscorthy.

On their return on Monday 1st May the garrison decided reluctantly to follow Pearse's orders and surrender to Colonel French who had the garrison shipped to Dublin to stand trial. As the British army entered Enniscorthy they were accompanied by Redmondites supporters who helped in seeking out sympathisers. It was estimated that the damage caused to the town amounted to the value of £3,500. In the county as a whole approximately 250 arrests were made of Republicans of whom only ten were convicted. Unlike Dublin, Enniscorthy was a bloodless revolution and only two civilians were wounded. Enniscorthy was the only town in the country that, like Dublin, rose up in rebellion.

IRISH REBELLION   MAY, 1916.

CAPT. JAMES RAFTER

JOHN ETCHINGHAM

CAPT. BRENNAN
ENNISCORTHY LEADERS.
Sentenced to Death ; sentence commuted to Five Years' Penal Servitude

These Shamrock-framed portraits are of officers who commanded the Irish Volunteer garrison at Enniscorthy.

The Rising that took place in Galway, like that in Dublin, lasted from Easter Monday, 24th April, until its dispersal on Saturday 29th April. When Liam Mellows assembled the Volunteers he was blessed with between 500 and 600 men at his command. What he was not blessed with was arms and ammunition. There are various conflicting numbers banded about but it appears that his garrison had between them a meagre 20 to 25 rifles and about 300 rounds for each rifle. There were 300 shotguns of differing ages and variety, an estimated 60 revolvers and the same number of pikes, the favourite weapon of Irish uprisings of the past. On Tuesday 25th April the Volunteers moved off with the planned attack of both the Clarinbridge and Oranmore police barracks. Apart from causing a little excitement at the two sites the attempt to capture them failed.

At dawn on Wednesday 26th April another group of Volunteers, who had camped overnight at the crossroads at Carnmore, noticed a patrol of several military vehicles leaving Galway city. The patrol headed directly for the Volunteers who were set up behind a covering wall. At about a hundred yards from the wall the convoy stopped, the police spilled from their vehicles firing constantly, and despite being given the order to return fire, such was the intensity of the initial police fire power that to take aim over the wall was tantamount to suicide.

Pressed to do so by his inspector, Constable Whelan shouted out "Surrender boys I know ye all" and was immediately shot dead. The same fate befell his inspector. The police returned to their cars after their flanking action was beaten off, then drove off in the direction of Oranmore. After this the Volunteers reassembled and made their way to Moyode where they holed up in an easily defended castle.

In Galway Bay a Royal Navy light cruiser H.M.S. *Gloucester* had been periodically shelling the fields surrounding the Athenry area. Rumours reached the Volunteers that the British army were gathering reinforcements for a final attack to end their resistance and that the *Gloucester* had already landed approximately a hundred Royal Marines. With the naval bombardment, fear of a overwhelming attack, shortage of food and arms the inevitable had to be faced. On Saturday 29th April the Volunteers dispersed, in most cases back to their homes, where many were later arrested. Mellows eventually managed to escape to New York.

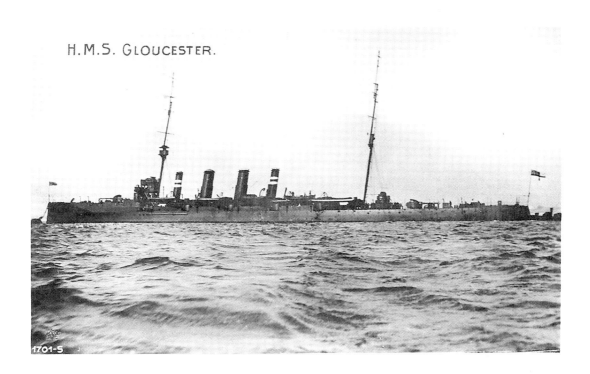

H.M.S. GLOUCESTER.

H.M.S. *Gloucester* on the high seas.

H.M.S. *Gloucester* was a Town Class light cruiser built by William Beardmore and Company and launched in October 1909. In 1914, under the command of Captain Kelly, she attacked and damaged the German cruiser *Breslau*. She was assigned to the Grand Fleet and in 1916 landed Royal Marines in Galway Bay during the Easter Rising. In June of that year she took part in the Battle of Jutland. However, there is some dispute as to whether it was H.M.S. *Gloucester* or H.M.S. *Laburnum*, an Acacia Class sloop, that shelled the Volunteers as both ships were known to be in the area at the time.

During the Rising County Cork saw little action until the early morning of Tuesday 2nd May. At Bawnard House, Castlelyons, lived the Kent family who were farmers. The family were also fierce nationalists and had for some years clashed with the local authorities. Several of the brothers prepared to take up arms in the Rising but the call never came. Fearing a police raid the brothers left the house on Tuesday 25th April, only returning when they believed it safe at the dead of night on 1st May. In the early hours of 2nd May a loud banging was heard at the door of the house that woke William, one of the brothers. Sticking his head out of the window his bleary eyes recognised the dark images of police uniforms. Thomas Kent was now awake and questioned the police who told him that they had arrest warrants for all the family. With that the police began a barrage of gunfire that left bullets in the walls and no pane of glass unshattered. The Kents were in an impossible position – the house was surrounded and they were outnumbered both in manpower and firepower.

With all the firearms they could muster, they gave as good as they got. The police's situation was looking unsure so army reinforcements were called up from the barracks in Fermoy. The fight was so one-sided that when David (another of the brothers) was wounded they surrendered.

The fight had lasted for three hours during which time many of the constables were wounded and the chief constable was killed by a bullet to his temple.

Ordered out of the house and stood against the wall, Thomas and William were handcuffed, Thomas not being given time to put on his boots. Richard seized the opportunity and made a dash for freedom, but was easily shot down. Both Richard and David were treated for their wounds by military medics before being sent to the military hospital in Fermoy.

Irish Rebellion, May, 1916.

Arrest of Edmund Kent. at 4 a.m.
He was subsequently shot.

This postcard shows Thomas Kent – *not* Edmund! – on the left and William Kent on the right, being taken into custody.

The 75 year old mother of the boys was comforted by the local priest Canon Peader O'Leary and transported to Fermoy Barracks where she was held for several hours before being released into the custody of her nephew. William and Thomas were taken by train to Cork and marched from the station to Cork Military Detention Barracks. On 4th May, Richard died of his wounds, and on the same day both Thomas and William were court martialled. William was acquitted but Thomas was sentenced to death. Richard's body was released to the family on the understanding that there was to be no show or display at his funeral. Despite this, people came out one last time to pay their respects as his body was escorted to the graveside. Thomas was executed by firing squad on 9th May, the only person executed outside of Dublin for their part in the uprising of 1916.

Chapter 6: Who's Who?

This chapter of the book depicts portraits of other, perhaps not so well-known persons who played their part in the struggle for Irish freedom at Easter 1916. There is no definitive catalogue of the postcards published on the subject of the Easter Rising. Every day 'new' postcards appear for sale on the internet and elsewhere. Sometimes these are part of a known set but sometimes it can be a previously unknown card. My comments on the postcards shown here are made on the basis of my experience gained over many years of collecting.

Allen, Thomas

IRISH REBELLION. MAY 1916

Lieutenant THOMAS ALLEN

('C' Coy., 1st Battalion, Irish Volunteers).

Shot in Action at Four Courts,

April 28th, 1916.

This out of focus photograph shows Allen in his Volunteers uniform and is taken from a photograph of four Volunteers in their uniform that included Thomas Fullam who fought at Bolland's Mill. Allen was a native of Moyvalley on the border between Co. Meath and Co. Kildare. He held the rank of lieutenant in the I.V. and fought in the Four Courts Garrison. He was wounded during the conflict and died at the age of 29 in Richmond Hospital on Saturday 29th April 1916, leaving a wife and three children.

Ashe, Thomas

Thomas Patrick Ashe was born in Kinard, Co. Kerry on 12th June 1885. He entered the De La Salle College in Waterford in 1905 and in 1908 began teaching at the Corduff National School, Lusk. Whilst there he founded the Black Raven Pipe Band and the Lusk G.A.A. Club. His strong Nationalist views led to him being recruited by the I.R.B. who in 1914 sent him to America on a fund-raising tour. After the Rising he was court martialled on 10th May and sentenced to death commuted to ten years penal servitude.

IRISH REBELLION, MAY 1916

THOMAS ASHE
(Leader of the North County Dublin Volunteers in the Rising),
Sentenced to Death;
Sentence commuted to Penal Servitude for Life.

He was sent to Lewes Prison during which time he wrote the poem *Let Me Carry Your Cross for Ireland, Lord*. After the general amnesty of June 1917 he returned to Ireland to work for the I.V. and Sinn Fein, travelling the country as a propagandist making speeches in defiance of the British authorities. He was eventually arrested in Ballinalee in August of that year and sentenced to two years hard labour for inciting the civilian population.

He was sent to Mountjoy Prison, Dublin where he demanded to be treated as a political prisoner, but having failed in this he went on hunger strike on 20th September 1917. In retaliation the authorities removed his boots and bedding and by the 23rd, having refused food for three days, he was force fed after which he collapsed. He was immediately sent to the Mater Hospital where it was discovered his lung had been punctured during his forced feeding. Two days later on 25th September he died of heart and lung failure.

His body lay in state at City Hall before a cortege, followed by an estimated 30,000 people, made its way through Dublin to Glasnevin. Michael Collins gave the oration, after which a firing party fired several salvos over the grave.

Rt. Hon. H.H. Asquith, Prime Minister.

Asquith, Henry Herbert

Herbert Henry Asquith was a Yorkshire man who was educated at Balliol College, Oxford and was called to the Bar in 1876. He entered Parliament in 1886 and took silk in 1890. He was to become Home Secretary in 1892 and Chancellor of the Exchequer in 1905. In 1908 he became Prime Minister and was forced into an alliance with the Irish Parliamentary Party thus enabling the third Home Rule Bill to be passed. As Prime Minister he led Britain into the First World War but resigned in 1916. Made a Peer in 1926, he died in February, 1928.

Barry, Tadhg

Barry was born in the Blarney Street area of Cork into a working class family. For four years he worked in Our Lady's Asylum until in 1909 he started working as a journalist on the *Cork Free Press*. He was a prominent member of the Cork I.T.G.W.U. and secretary to the Cork branch of Sinn Fein. In 1913 he joined the I.V. In 1917 he was arrested for a seditious speech. Whilst in prison he went on hunger strike and was released, only to be arrested again under the German Plot. In 1919 he became branch secretary of the I.T.G.W.U. and in 1920 was elected an Alderman of Cork City. Later in the year he was arrested again and sent to Ballykinlar Internment Camp, Co. Down where on 15th November 1921 he was shot by a sentry. His funeral was the largest seen in Cork which closed for the day. It was attended by representatives from all the cities in Ireland, by bishops, T.D.s and Michael Collins.

TADHG BARRY.

Rt. Hon. Augustine Birrell, M. P.

PHOTO REGINALD HAINES

E.B.51.

Birrell, Augustine

Augustine Birrell was Chief Secretary to Ireland from 1908 until 1916. A Liberal politician, he had great affection for the Irish and Ireland, especially the Nationalists, and was not adverse to poking fun at the Ulster Unionists, endearing him to the Nationalists. He espoused Ireland's cause in the Cabinet and was instrumental in passing acts that were favourable to Ireland but was criticised for spending too much time in London. His defence was that his Cabinet duties necessitated him being there.

Brugha, Cathal

The son of a Yorkshireman, Brugha was christened Charles Burgess and was educated at Belvedere College, Dublin. On leaving school he entered into partnership in a candle making company. Embracing his Irishness he changed his name to the Gaelic form and joined the Gaelic League, the Gaelic Athletic Association and finally the Irish Volunteers. During the Rising his bravery stood out, for which it is said he received a score of bullet wounds which left him partially lame. Such was his condition that he was not court martialled or imprisoned as he was not expected to live.

Elected President of the first Dail and later Minister for National Defence, he was the most venomous opponent of the Treaty. When the Four Courts fell during the Civil War he went to the Hammam Hotel to continue the fight, eventually ordering his men to make an exit for safety when the position became hopeless. He then came from the building guns blazing and was shot and fatally wounded. Small in stature his bravery knew no bounds though some thought him foolhardy. He died on 7th July 1922.

410 A   SIR. E. H. CARSON, K.C., M.P.   ROTARY PHOTO. E.C.

Carson, Sir Edward

On 9th February 1854 Edward Henry Carson was born into a wealthy Anglican-Dublin family. He read law at Trinity College, Dublin, gaining a BA and MA before beginning a glittering career as a barrister. He was called to the Bar in 1877 and was appointed Q.C. in 1889. In 1892 he became Solicitor General for Ireland and in 1895 won the libel case brought by Oscar Wilde against the Marquess of Queensbury. In 1900 he was made Solicitor General for England and knighted. His political career was no less glittering. He took up the cause of Ulster's opposition to the 3rd Home Rule Bill, urging their independence with the formation of the Ulster Volunteer Force, and was the first to sign the Ulster Covenant on 28th September 1912.

Casement, Sir Roger

Roger David Casement was born on 1st September 1864 in Sandycove. He received his knighthood in 1911 for his humanitarian work highlighting the plight of indigenous natives in the Congo and Peru. In 1913, when he retired from British Colonial Service, he took up the cause of Irish Nationalism, though he had in fact been a member of the Gaelic League since 1904. In 1913 he helped form the I.V. and was instrumental in organising gunrunning from Howth. He travelled to Germany with the aim of raising an Irish regiment from Irish P.O.W.s. He failed in his task and returned to Ireland in a German submarine, landing on Banna Strand. He was soon arrested and sent to London for trial where he was convicted of treason. The high profile case against him weighed heavily on his "Black Diaries" that alluded to his homosexuality. He was hanged in Pentonville Prison, London, on 3rd August 1916 and buried in the grounds of the prison. His body was repatriated to Ireland in 1965 where he was given a state funeral.

SIR ROGER CASEMENT.

EAMONN CEANNT
(Commandant of the South Dublin Area),
Executed May 8th, 1916.
One of the signatories of the "Irish Republic Proclamation."

Ceannt, Eamonn

Ceannt, the son of an R.I.C. officer, was brought up in Dublin and worked in the treasury department of Dublin Corporation. He joined the Gaelic League and was an honorary secretary of Sinn Fein and founder member of the Irish Volunteers. A skilled piper, he helped form the Dublin Pipers Club and was granted a private audience with Pope Pius X for whom he played the Uileann pipes. His command during the Rising was to control the South Dublin Union, a series of hospitals and other buildings that spread over a wide area, which he managed to do until the end of the Rising with the aid of his very able second in command, Cathal Brugha.

Childers, Erskine

Childers was born in England but brought up in Ireland and was the author of *Riddle of the Sands*. In 1919 he was elected to the Dail as member for Kildare-Wicklow and in 1921 he was in London as an adviser to the Irish delegation during the Peace negotiations. An anti-Treaty supporter, he acted as their propaganda chief. In 1922 he was arrested at the home of his cousin, Robert Barton, for carrying a gun given to him by Michael Collins. Carrying a gun was a crime against the Public Safety Act and for this he was executed on 24th November 1922. His son, Erskine Hamilton Childers, became President of the Irish Republic in 1973.

ERSKINE CHILDERS
Died for Ireland, 24th November, 1922.

PETER CLANCY (Co. Clare),
Sentenced to Death,
Sentence commuted to 10 Years' Penal Servitude.

Clancy, Peter

A grainy photograph of Clancy who like so many is buried in Glasnevin Cemetery. Peter Clancy, more popularly known as Peadar, was born in Cranny, Co. Clare and came to Dublin in 1913. He fought in the Church Street Bridge area which was part of Four Courts Garrison in 1916. After his release in 1917 he was a partner in "The Republican Outfitters" in Talbot Street. He was arrested in April 1920 and led a hunger strike of about 100 prisoners in Mountjoy Prison. He was Vice Commandant of the I.R.A. Dublin Brigade. In the early hours of Sunday 21st November 1921, Bloody Sunday, together with Dick McKee and Conor Clune, he was taken to Dublin Castle where both were severely beaten and killed.

THOMAS J. CLARKE,
Executed May 3rd, 1916.
One of the signatories of the "Irish Republic Proclamation."

Clarke, Thomas

There would have been no Rising were it not for Clarke. Born in the Isle of Wight, his father was a serving soldier in the British army. He emigrated to America where he joined Clan na Gael and agreed to return to England under the name of Hammond Wilson to carry out dynamite attacks. Before he could carry out his mission he was arrested and spent the next fifteen years in British prisons where he was harshly treated. During his time in prison be befriended John Daly and upon his release Clarke went to the Daly household in Limerick where he met Kathleen, Daly's niece, whom he eventually married. The married couple went to America where Clarke took up again with Clan na Gael. After seven years the couple returned to Ireland where they bought a newsagent and tobacconist in Amiens Street, Dublin. Clarke set about the task of revitalising the moribund I.R.B. His is the first name on the Irish Republic Proclamation.

Colbert, Cornelius

Con Colbert was born near Newcastle West, Co. Limerick and educated at the Athea National School. At the age of sixteen he joined his sister who lived in Ranelagh, Co. Dublin and continued his education at the Christian Brothers in North Richmond Street, Dublin. Short of stature he was a deeply religious man fond of wearing the kilt and worked as a clerk at Limerick Railway Station and in Kennedy's Bakery in Dublin. In 1908 he met Sean Heuston, joined Na Fianna Eireann and served on its council for several years. Patrick Pearse employed him at St. Enda's as a drill instructor. He was a member of both the I.V. and the I.R.B. In the weeks leading up to the Rising part of his duties was to act as Thomas Clarke's bodyguard.

Cornelius Colbert

MacDonagh's arrival with the surrender was both a surprise and disappointment to him and the garrison and they were marched under military guard to Richmond Barracks. It is believed his court martial was held on Thursday 4th May after which he was moved to Kilmainham. On Sunday 7th May he was informed of his sentence of execution, to be carried out the following morning. Before Colbert's execution a soldier asked for his right hand, which he complied with and the man shook it warmly. Cornelius Colbert was executed on Monday 8th May.

Coleman, Richard

Richard Coleman was born at Swords in 1890 and was educated locally. At one time he had ambitions for the priesthood. He worked as a railway clerk in both Galway and Cavan, then as an agent for the Prudential Insurance Co. He joined Sinn Fein and in 1914 was made captain of the Volunteers in Swords. He fought with Ashe before being ordered to Dublin. After the surrender of the garrison he was court martialled and sent to Dartmoor Prison, then Lewes Prison and released in the amnesty of June 1917. One of the founding members of the New Ireland Friendly Society he was arrested in Ennis campaigning for De Valera for wearing his Volunteers uniform. He was sent to Mountjoy Prison where he joined in with Ashe's hunger strike and then to Dundalk Prison. Eventually released he was re-arrested under the German Plot. On 17th May 1918 he was imprisoned at Usk Prison, Monmouthshire. Here he contacted influenza and then pneumonia due to his weakened state of health. On 2nd December his condition was so bad he was moved to the prison hospital where on 7th December he died. His funeral was held in Dublin where an estimated crowd of 15,000 mourners followed the coffin and a firing party of six fired three volleys over his grave.

Connolly, James

James Connolly was a Scot who joined the British army to escape poverty but deserted and took a variety of jobs that formed his socialist outlook. He went to America where he became involved with socialist movements and was eventually enticed back to Dublin as assistant to Jim Larkin, the charismatic leader of the Irish Transport and General Workers Union. When Larkin left for America Connolly became the union's general secretary. One of his first actions was to raise the Citizen Army, a paramilitary force, to protect striking members of the union who in the Dublin General Lock Out of 1913 were set upon and severely beaten by thugs hired by the bosses.

He is claimed to have said to his men before the Rising "But, if we should win hold on to your rifles … we're not only for political liberty but for economical liberty also". To achieve his socialist aims he was prepared to start a Rising of his own. Rumours of his plans reached the ears of the I.R.B. and it was for this reason that he was "kidnapped" by them and let into the plans they had laid down for a Rising. Connolly was appointed Commandant of the Dublin forces. Whilst stepping out of the G.P.O. to check on orders he had given, he was hit by a ricocheting bullet that shattered his left ankle which left him stretchered. He was held in a room in Dublin Castle where he wrote his terms of surrender. On 7th of May, unable to stand, he was sat on a chair for his execution in the stone breakers yard.

IRISH REBELLION, MAY 1916.

JAMES CONNOLLY,
(Commandant-General Dublin Division),
Executed May 9th, 1916.
One of the signatories of the "Irish Republic Proclamation."

SEAN CONNOLLY,
(Irish Republican Army),
Killed in Action at City Hall, Dublin, Easter Monday, 1916.

Connolly, Sean

Sean Connolly (no relative of James Connolly) was a captain in the Citizens Army. An aspiring actor with a growing reputation, he was already connected to the Abbey Theatre. It was on the roof of City Hall, leading a party of the Citizens Army, that Connolly gained the dubious distinction of being the first man to die for his country in its bid for independence.

Cosgrave, William Thomas

William Thomas (Liam) Cosgrave was born at James's Street, Dublin on 6th June 1880 and educated by the Christian Brothers at Merino. He attended the first Sinn Fein Convention in 1905 and in 1909 was elected as a Sinn Fein candidate in the local Dublin elections. In 1913 he joined the Irish Volunteers and served with Ceannt in his South Dublin Union Brigade. After his release from Frongoch he was elected as M.P. for Kilkenny in 1917 and again in 1918. In the first Dail of 1919 he was appointed as Minister of Local Government, a post in which he was very successful. Though a friend of de Valera he supported the Treaty and in 1922 he became the first Prime Minister of the Irish Free State, an office he held for ten years. In 1923 his home was burnt down by the I.R.A. and in the same year he formed and became the leader of the new party Cumann na nGaedheal. He lost the 1932 election and in 1933, with three other parties, formed Fine Gael and served as its leader and leader of the opposition until his retirement from public life in 1944. He died on 16th November 1965 and after a state funeral was buried in Goldenbridge Cemetery, Inchicore.

CAPTAIN WILLIAM COSGRAVE, T.C.
(DUBLIN)
Sentenced to Death.
Commuted to Penal Servitude for Life.

SEAN COSTELLO (Athlone),
2nd Lieutenant I. V.,
Died from wound received in Action while on Despatch Duty
At Bolands' Mills.

Costello, Sean

Costello, seen looking smart in his Volunteers' uniform, was born in Cornamagh on the outskirts of Athlone where he worked locally. He was a founder member of the I.V. and during the Rising was wounded and taken to Sir Patrick Dunn's Hospital where he died on Wednesday 26th April 1916.

Daly, John

John Daly was born in Limerick on 18th October 1845 into a fiercely Fenian family. He started his working life in a wood yard with his father and soon joined the I.R.B. He and his brother Edward (father of Edward Daly) were arrested for making munitions in 1866. He led the Limerick section of the ill-fated Rising of 1867, eventually taking his men to attack the police barracks at Kilmallock. After this he fled to America. On his return to Ireland in 1869 he fought for the release of Fenian prisoners. In 1883 he moved to Birmingham, where he was betrayed whilst carrying a parcel of explosives. Whilst in prison he befriended Thomas Clarke and when he was released campaigned for Clarke's release. Back in Limerick he was elected as M.P. for Limerick City in the election of 1895 only to be disqualified as a treason felon. The following year he went on a lecture tour of America. Daly was elected Mayor of Limerick three times during which time he had the Royal Coat of Arms removed from the Town Hall. He founded a successful bakery business in the city before his death on 30th June 1916. This is a photograph of a young John Daly, whose beard in later life was longer and white.

JOHN DALY (Fenian).

65

Daly, Edward

Edward Daly (seen here in his Volunteers uniform), was also known as Ned, and was the brother-in-law of Tom Clarke and the nephew of John Daly. The son of a famous Limerick Fenian family, his father died five months before he was born. Edward Daly, a member of the I.R.B., was Commandant of the 1st Dublin Battalion that was charged with holding the Four Courts area of the city where much fierce combat occurred. This included Jameson's Distillery and North King Street where hand to hand fighting took place. Within Daly's command was the Mendicity Institute, a charity home for the destitute that had been established in 1818. Here the 25 year old Sean Houston and his small band of Volunteers controlled Kingsbridge Station (now Houston Station) for three days, preventing hundreds of British reinforcements joining the Dublin troops.

E. DALY
(Commandant of the North-West Dublin Area),
Executed May 4th, 1916.

ED. de VALERA
(Commandant of the Ringsend Area),
Sentenced to Death;
Sentence commuted to Penal Servitude for Life.

de Valera, Eamon

Eamon de Valera, the man who guided a fledgling Irish Free State, was born in America but grew up in Ireland, becoming a maths teacher and joining the Volunteers. He became Commandant Dublin 3rd. Battalion that covered Boland's Mills, Westland Row Station, Mount Street Bridge and Northumberland Road, the scene of the bloodiest battle of the Rising. His battalion was set to pulling up railway lines amongst other actions. He was saved execution by the fact of his birth, going on to head a secret government, lead the fight for Irish Independence, split the country and cause more murder and mayhem in the years to come but outlast all to see peace and earn his place as a founding father of an independent Ireland.

MICHAEL D. DeLACY
(Enniscorthy Volunteers),
Sentenced to Death,
Sentence commuted to Penal Servitude for Five Years.

DeLacy, Michael D.

Michael DeLacy was known locally as 'Professor DeLacy' as he taught at Knockbeg College, one of Ireland's oldest schools. DeLacy held the rank of captain in the Enniscorthy Volunteer company. He was one of the leaders of the Enniscorthy rebellion and a signatory to the surrender of the town. Together with the town's other leaders he was sent to Dublin for trial and on Monday 15th May he was sentenced to death; however, the sentence was commuted to five years penal service.

Devoy, John

John Devoy was born in 1842 at Johnstown, Co. Kildare. A Fenian from his early years he joined the French Foreign Legion to gain military experience. Back in Ireland in 1862 he was an I.R.B. organiser in Naas. With the arrest of the I.R.B. leadership he assumed control of the Brotherhood until his arrest in 1866. He gained early release but was exiled to America, where he joined Clan na Gael, published Republican newspapers and organised the escape from prison of Fenians in Freemantle, Australia. Through his American network he raised funds to support Pearse's school, St. Endas, his financial clout helping to bankroll the Rising. He broke with de Valera and the I.R.B. in 1920 and supported the Treaty. The man who British authorities considered at one time to be their most dangerous revolutionary died in America on 28th September 1928.

JOHN DEVOY (Fenian).

CAPTAIN F. FAHY,

Who was Command'ant in the Four Courts.

Fahy, Francis Patrick

Francis Patrick Fahy was born in Kilchreest, Co. Galway. He taught in Tralee, was a board member of the G.A.A. and the county secretary of the Gaelic League. He joined the I.V and took part in the Howth gun running and was appointed captain of C Company 1st Battalion, Dublin Brigade. His wife served alongside him at the Four Courts. After his release in 1917 he was re-arrested under the German Plot. In 1918 he was elected to the first Dail for South Galway, a seat he held for 35 years. From 1932 until 1951 he was Chairman of the Dail. He died in Ranelagh, Dublin on 12th July 1953.

This is Fahy in his robes collecting his BA in 1901. The caption states "Commandant in the Four Courts", but this is incorrect as it was Edward Daly who was the Four Courts Commandant.

DESMOND FITZGERALD.

Sentenced to 20 Years.

Sentence Commuted to 10 Years.

Fitzgerald, Desmond

Desmond Fitzgerald was a journalist, politician and student of the Irish language. An organiser of the Volunteers in Kerry, he fought in the G.P.O. during the Rising. He was elected as a Sinn Fein member in Co. Dublin in the first Dail and held several posts including Director of Propaganda during the War of Independence. Afterwards he held several posts including Minister for Foreign Affairs and Minister of Defence in 1927. Later he sat in the Senate. His son Garret, born in 1926, became leader of Fine Gael.

Galligan, Paul

PETER PAUL GALLIGAN

Peter Paul Galligan was born on 20th June 1888 at Carrigallen, Co. Leitrim, one of four sons. His mother died when he was at an early age and the family moved to Drumnalaragh Co. Cavan, the home town of his father. Galligan was a religious man throughout his life. He joined the I.V. which led to him being recruited into the I.R.B. After surrendering at Enniscorthy he was sent to Lewes Prison. In the 1918 election he stood unopposed as the Sinn Fein candidate for Cavan West. He was arrested in September 1920 and elected as a Sinn Fein T.D. for Cavan in 1921. He supported the Treaty. In 1922 he retired from politics and ran a successful gents clothing shop in Henry Street and a warehousing business in Dublin. He died in Dublin on 14th December 1966. His funeral was attended by Sean Lemass and Eamon de Valera and his tricolour draped coffin was given a military escort.

Gifford, Grace

Grace Gifford was born on 4th March 1888 into a comfortable family of twelve children in the fashionable area of Rathmines. She was brought up a Protestant and studied at the Dublin Metropolitan School of Art where she studied under Sir William Orpen who considered her one of his most able students; she eventually went on to study at the Slade School of Art in London. It was at the opening of St. Enda's School at Ranelagh that she met Joseph Mary Plunkett. Grace converted to Roman Catholicism in 1916 before her marriage to Plunkett. They were married in Kilmainham prison chapel on the evening of Plunkett's execution. During the Civil War she held a strongly anti-Treaty view for which she spent time in Kilmainham. It was while in prison that she painted a virgin and child on her cell wall which became known as the Kilmainham Madonna. At the end of the Civil War she struggled to earn a living, but gradually picked up commissions and managed to pay her way. She was ostracised by her in-laws who settled out of court over her husband's will. Grace never re-married and by the 1950s her health was failing. On 13th December 1955 she died at South Richmond Street, Dublin. She is buried in the Republican plot in Glasnevin Cemetery. President Sean T. O'Kelly attended her funeral.

IRISH REBELLION, MAY, 1916.

MRS. JOSEPH PLUNKETT
(MISS GRACE GIFFORD),
Who Married Joseph Plunkett in Kilmainham Prison a few hours
before his Execution on May 3rd, 1916.

Guest, Ivor Churchill

Ivor Churchill Guest, who became 1st Viscount Wimborne, was born in Wimborne House, London on 16th January 1873. He was educated at Eton and Trinity College Cambridge and fought in the 2nd Boer War. In 1900 he was elected M.P. for Plymouth and in 1910 made a Peer. In 1915 he was appointed Lord Lieutenant of Ireland and at the outbreak of the Easter Rising he declared Martial Law. He was exonerated over the failure of the government to recognise the signs of the Easter Rising and remained as Lord Lieutenant until 1918. He died on 14th June 1939 in the house in which he had been born.

IRISH REBELLION, MAY, 1916.

DR. RICHARD F. HAYES,
(Medical Officer, Lusk, Co. Dublin),
Sentenced to 20 Years' Penal Servitude.

Hayes, Richard Francis

Richard Francis Hayes was born in Bruree, Co. Limerick in 1878 and was educated locally where he was a school friend of Eamon de Valera. He joined the Volunteers and after qualifying as a doctor practised in Lusk, Co. Dublin. Initially he was second in command of Thomas Ashe's 5th Fingal Battalion but stepped down when Richard Mulcahy joined it and instead concentrated on supplying medical support to it. He was elected as T.D. for East Limerick in the first Dail and was a Treaty supporter but resigned from politics in 1924 to concentrate on his medical practice.

He became an expert on Irish historical issues, writing many books on the subject and was an Irish film censor from 1940 until 1954 during which time he was also a director of the Abbey Theatre. He died in 1958.

Heuston, John

John or Sean Heuston was a railway clerk in Limerick and organiser of Na Fianna Eireann (Irish Boy Scouts). He was a founder member of the Volunteers and worked with Con Colbert at St. Enda's in drilling the pupils. For almost 72 hours his band of Volunteers in the Mendicity Institution held up much needed British reinforcements. When it surrendered through lack of ammunition the British could not believe the small size of the garrison that had kept them at bay for so long. He was court martialled on Thursday 4th May and then taken to Kilmainham. It was not until Sunday 7th May that he was told of the court's verdict that he was to be executed the following day. Once informed of his fate, Heuston requested a visit from his mother, Sister Theresa, his aunt and his brother John who was training to become a Dominican brother. After his family had left, he was taken into the yard early on the morning of Monday 8th May where he was blindfolded and handcuffed and told to sit on a box. There then followed a volley of shots. Heuston's fight was over. Kingsbridge Station was renamed after him in 1966.

J. J. HEUSTON,
One of the leaders of the Rebellion,
Executed May 8th, 1916.

CAPTAIN THOMAS HUNTER,
Sentenced to Death.

Commuted to Penal Servitude for Life.

Hunter, Thomas

Thomas Hunter was born at Castletownroche, Co. Cork. Moving to Dublin in 1907 to train as an apprentice draper he joined the I.V. and was inducted in the I.R.B. He fought at Jacob's Biscuit Factory and was sent to Lewes Prison. Released in June 1917 he was re-arrested under the German Plot. He was also a partner in The Republican Outfitters and in 1918 was elected as Sinn Fein M.P. for North East Cork whilst in prison. He went on hunger strike several times. He retained his seat as a Sinn Fein T.D. in the first Dail but voted against the Treaty. During the Civil War he acted as quartermaster for the Cork Brigade. After a long illness he died at his home at Glanworth, Co. Cork on 11th March 1932.

Keating, Con

Con Keating was a native of Renard near Cahirciveen and joined the I.V. An expert radio operator, together with six other men he was sent to remove the British radio station on Valencia Island. On the night of Holy Thursday, 20th April, the car in which he was travelling took a wrong turn and plunged off the pier at Ballykissane, Co. Kerry near Killorgin into the River Laune. Of the four men in the car only the driver survived.

The two other men drowned in the car were Donal Sheehan and Charlie Monaghan. The bodies of Keating and Sheehan were found the following day. Monaghan's body was discovered six months later. The driver of the car, Thomas McInerney, was arrested and sent to Frongoch. He died during the War of Independence in Co. Tipperary.

CON KEATING.
DROWNED GOOD FRIDAY, 1916.
One of the occupants of the Motor Car going to Kerry. At the River Laune,
Killorglin, the motor turned off the main road and fell into the river.

THOS. R. KENT

Kent, Thomas

Thomas Kent was one of seven brothers and was born into a fiercely Nationalist family on 29th August 1865. The family lived at Bawnard House, Castlelyons, Co. Cork. He was a Gaelic League member and later joined the Irish Volunteers. Fearing arrest after the Rising he left his home, eventually returning on 2nd May. That evening the police came with warrants for the family and a gunfight ensued; eventually, hopelessly outnumbered, he and his brothers surrendered. He was taken to Cork Military Detention Barracks where on 4th May he was court martialled and sentenced to death. He was executed on 9th May by a squad of King's Own Scottish Borderers, fulfilling his request that no Irishman should be part of the firing squad.

Lawless, Frank

FRANK J. LAWLESS

Frank Lawless was born on 10th October 1870 at Saucerstown, Co. Dublin and was a well-respected member of the farming community. A strong Nationalist he joined both Sinn Fein and the Gaelic League in their early stages of existence. He and his son Joe fought together at Ashbourne. After the surrender he was sent to Lewes Prison. Soon after his release he was re-arrested under the German Plot, an alleged plot between Sinn Fein and Germany that led to the arrest of most of the senior members of Sinn Fein. Like Coleman he was sent to Usk Prison. Whilst in prison he stood for election and was released for the day to hear the result of the election, which he won. He was a T.D. in both the first and second Dail and voted to ratify the Treaty. He died on 16th April 1922 from injuries sustained from an accident and was buried with full military honours at Killossery Cemetery, Rolestown.

Lowe, William Henry Muir

William Lowe was born in the North West Province, India on 20th October 1861. His father, William Henry, was an official of the Indian Civil Service. His mother's maiden name was Charlotte Muir. In 1881 he passed out of Sandhurst and was commissioned in the 7th Dragoon Guards. The following year he fought in the Egyptian Campaign, where he was awarded two campaign medals. In 1895 he married Frances Broster with whom he had a son, William, and a daughter, Elizabeth, who became a nun. In 1886 he was sent to Burma for a year where he received further awards and was promoted to captain in 1887 and five years later to major. Further promotion came in 1899 when he was made lieutenant colonel assuming command of the 7th Dragoon Guards. During the Second Boer War he took control of his regiment and in 1900 was made honorary colonel. Here he was mentioned twice in despatches and awarded two medals. In March 1903 he was appointed quartermaster general of Southern Command and promoted to a full colonel. In 1905 he was colonel in charge of Northern Command records and officer for the Imperial Yeomanry. A year later he was made Companion of the Bath. In 1908 he retired only to join up again in 1914 with the rank of brigadier general and placed as commander of the 3rd Reserve Cavalry Brigade at Curragh. At the outbreak of the Rising he ordered his troops to Dublin where he took command of British forces until the surrender by Patrick Pearse. He finally retired from the army in 1919 and died at the age of 88 in London on 7th February 1944.

FINIAN LYNCH, B.A.,
(Captain, Irish Volunteers),
Sentenced to Death;
Sentence Commuted to 10 Years' Penal Servitude.

Lynch, Finian

This photograph shows Lynch in his graduation robes when he received his B.A. in 1913. Fionan or Finian Lynch was born in Caherciveen, Co. Kerry. A founder member of the I.V. he later joined the I.R.B. He fought in the Four Courts Garrison during the Rising. After his release from prison in 1917 he was elected as the Sinn Fein M.P. for Kerry South and then to the first Dail. A close friend of Collins he was a Treaty supporter and rose to the rank of brigadier in the National Army during the Civil War. He held the portfolios of Education and later Fisheries during his political career from which he retired when he qualified as a barrister in 1938. He was made a circuit court judge in 1944 and died on 3rd June 1966.

SEAN MAC DIARMADA,
Executed May 9th, 1916.
One of the signatories of the "Irish Republic Proclamation."

MacDiarmada, Sean

Sean MacDiarmada, also known as MacDermott, was born in Co. Leitrim and had little formal education. After spending some time in Scotland he returned to Belfast taking various jobs, and there he met Bulmer Hobson. Soon after, he joined the I.R.B. and became a full-time paid organiser. He was now travelling the length and breadth of the country, like St. Paul spreading the Good Word of independence and Nationalism. He came to the attention of Clarke and soon the two became inseparable as mentor and pupil. In 1911 he was struck with polio and thereafter had to rely on a walking stick. He was arrested and sentenced to prison for four months in 1915 for contravening the Defence of the Realm Act. His effort during the Rising accounts for little; it was his ceaseless work before that has written his name into history.

MacDonagh, Thomas

When Thomas MacDonagh joined the Gaelic League he was a teacher who later taught at St. Enda's and then lectured at University College Dublin. He was a founder member of the Volunteers, where he was director of training, and of the secret military council of the I.R.B. He assisted in organising the Howth gun running and the O'Donovan Rossa funeral.

A signatory of the Proclamation, he was Commandant of approximately 140 men of the 2nd. Battalion which took control of Jacob's Biscuit Factory and the surrounding area. From the upper floors of the building the garrison had a wide field of fire into Portobello Barracks and Dublin Castle. It was not until Sunday 1st April, after consulting with Ceannt, that he and Ceannt both surrendered.

THOMAS MacDONAGH
(Commandant of Bishop Street Area),
Executed May 3rd, 1916.
of the signatories the "Irish Republic Proclamation."

EOIN MacNEILL, B.A.,
(President Irish Volunteers),
Sentenced by Courtmartial to Penal Servitude for Life.

MacNeill, Eoin

Eoin (John) MacNeill was born on 15th May 1867 in Co. Antrim and was educated in Belfast. His deep interest in Irish history led him to become one of the founders of the Gaelic League. By 1908 he was Professor of Early Irish History at University College, Dublin. At The O'Rahilly's invitation MacNeill wrote *The North Began*, an article that led to the formation of the Irish Volunteers; he later served in the Volunteers as Chief of Staff. He was opposed to armed rebellion and after discovering the Rising plot did all he could to stop it. For his non-active part in the Rising he was imprisoned and upon release stood as a Sinn Fein candidate in Dail Eireann. He was pro-Treaty and eventually became Minister for Education. He died in Dublin aged 78 on 25th October 1945.

JAMES MALINN
(Irish Republican Army).
Sentenced to Death. Sentence commuted to
10 Years Penal Servitude.

Malinn, James

James Malinn was the proprietor of a gents barber shop on Eden Quay and lived across the Liffey at 19 George's Quay. In 1914 he was arrested for stealing a soldier's rifle while the soldier was in his shop having a haircut. He was acquitted of the charge, but after the Rising he was arrested again and held at Richmond Barracks before being deported to Wakefield Prison on 6th May where he was appointed "Local Intelligence Officer", his barber's chair being a good conduit for receiving and passing on information.

Mallin, Michael

Mallin was a Dubliner and lived at Emmet Road, Inchicore. After his schooling, he joined the British Army. An accomplished musician, he was the leader of the Leon Fedderstone Orchestra but earned his living as a silk weaver, eventually becoming the secretary of the Weavers Union. It was through his union connections that he met James Connolly and joined the Citizens Army, becoming its Chief of Staff. Under his command a contingent of the Citizen Army seized St. Stephen's Green. When British machine guns fired on them from the top floors of the Shelbourne Hotel, Mallin withdrew his troops to the safety of the Royal College of Surgeons building where on Sunday 30th April he surrendered to Major de Courcy Wheeler. Michael Mallin and his second-in-command, Countess Markievicz, were taken under military guard to Richmond Barracks. Mallin was tried at the barracks on Friday 5th May, then transferred to Kilmainham where on Sunday 7th May he was informed that he was to be executed the following morning. In his cell that evening he was visited by his pregnant wife and their four children. After this tearful goodbye Mallin's execution was carried out at 3.45 a.m. on the morning of Monday 8th May.

MICHAEL MALLIN,
(Commandant Irish Republican Army),
Executed May 8th, 1916.

COUNTESS MARKIEVICZ,
(Who took a prominent part in the Rebellion, Stephen's Green Area),
Sentenced to Death;
Sentence commuted to Penal Servitude for Life.

Markievicz, Countess

Constance Gore-Booth was born in London and brought up at Lissadell House, Co. Sligo. Considered a beautiful headstrong girl after her coming out she went to Paris to study art where she met and married an impoverished Polish count. Soon after the birth of their daughter they returned to Ireland, but quickly separated. Constance took up the cause of Irish independence and helped to form Fianna na Eireann (the Irish boy scouts). She fought with Michael Mallin during the Rising and was sentenced to prison at Holloway Womens' Prison, London. She was the first woman elected to the U.K. House of Commons, but never took her seat, and went on to hold the cabinet post of Minister of Labour in the first Dáil Éireann (the Irish Parliament). Ever the rebel, she sided with the anti-Treaty forces during the Civil War. In 1927, a month after being re-elected to the Dail, she died of cancer and was buried at Glasnevin Cemetery.

Maxwell, General Sir John Grenfell

General Sir John Grenfell Maxwell was born in Liverpool on 11th July 1859 into a Scottish Protestant family and went to school in Cheltenham and then to Sandhurst Military Academy. He joined the Black Watch and served in the Egyptian Campaign where he commanded the 2nd Egyptian Brigade at Omdurman, after which he was made Governor of Nubia and then Omdurman. Kitchener commandeered him to take charge of the 14th Brigade during the Boer War where he was later made Military Governor of Pretoria. For his loyal service he was awarded the Knight Commander of the Most Loyal Order of the Bath and Companion of the Order of St. Michael and St. George. He later returned to Egypt as Commander of the Army of Occupation. From semi-retirement he was called to take control of the "Irish situation" and arrived in Dublin in the early hours of Friday 28th April where he was given a free hand to put down the Rising. As a soldier he employed martial law as he set about the trials of the leaders in camera and devoid of a jury or defence counsel. The speed at which the sentences of execution were carried out caused alarm to Prime Minister Asquith and the British Government before he was pressurised to stop further executions. Maxwell earned the sobriquet of "Bloody Maxwell" from the Irish for his order of the executions. Maxwell's time in Ireland was short-lived for by the end of the year he was Commander-in-Chief for the Northern Command in York. He retired in 1922 and died on 21st February 1929.

NO REST FOR THAT BRUTE MAXWELL!

McBride, John

John McBride was born in Westport Co. Mayo in 1868. When barely twenty he joined the I.R.B. but soon found the organisation moribund and left it. In Dublin he joined the Celtic Literary Society and befriended Arthur Griffith. He decided to try his luck in South Africa and worked for the Rand Mining Corporation as an assayer. In 1897 Griffith joined him and they organised the Centenary Celebrations of the Rising of the United Irishmen. With Arthur Lynch, an Australian born Nationalist, they formed the pro-Boer Irish Brigade which served in several engagements of the Boer War. By 1900 he was back in Ireland and stood unsuccessfully for the South Mayo constituency. Later that year at the International Exhibition in Paris he met Maud Gonne. The following year he was in New York where he acted as the best man at the wedding of Thomas Clarke and Kathleen Daly. His own wedding day came on 23rd February 1903 when he married Maud Gonne in Paris, with whom he had a son Sean. The marriage did not last and they were legally separated in 1905. McBride returned to Ireland and resumed his I.R.B. membership and joined the I.V. Whilst he was not privy to the Easter Rising plans, when he realised it was happening he offered his services to MacDonagh and joined his 2nd Dublin Battalion at the Jacob's Biscuit Factory Garrison.

MAJOR JOHN McBRIDE
(Born in Westport. May 7th, 1868).
Executed in Kilmainham Prison. May 5th. 1916.

J. J. Walsh]   DOCTOR McCARTAN.   [Dublin
(After his passage as a stoker on a tramp steamer to present the Irish Claim to America).

McCartan, Patrick

Patrick McCartan was born on 13th March 1978 near Carrickmore, Co. Tyrone. As a young man he emigrated to America where he joined Clan na Gael and edited *Irish Freedom*. Returning to Ireland he qualified as a doctor and joined the I.R.B. After the Rising (which he did not take part in due to the countermanding order) he was sent to prison in England. Upon his release he worked to get Sinn Fein candidates elected until he was himself elected in 1918 for King's County. He was a member of the first Dail and appointed Sinn Fein Representative in America. In 1921 he was re-elected to the Dail for Leix-Offaly. He reluctantly supported the Treaty but soon after retired from politics until 1945 when he stood for the Presidency. In 1948 he was made a Senator, a post he held till 1951. He died on 26th March 1963.

JOHN F. McENTEE
(Command :nt, Louth).
SENTENCED TO DEATH.
Sentence commuted to Penal Servitude for Life.

McEntee, John

John McEntee, who was better known as Sean, was born in Belfast where he qualified as an electrical engineer. For his part in the Rising he served in three English prisons. He was elected Sinn Fein M.P. for South Monaghan and was opposed to the Treaty. Treasurer of Sinn Fein he founded Fianna Fail with de Valera and held many executive government positions including that of Deputy Prime Minister (1959-65) before retiring from politics in 1969. He published his experiences of the Rising in his book *Episode at Easter*. John McEntee died on 10th January 1984.

JOSEPH McGUINNESS,
(Sentenced to 3 years imprisonment)
CANDIDATE FOR SOUTH LONGFORD, MAY, 1917.

McGuinness, Joseph

This is not a postcard but a piece of card the size of a postcard with the portrait of Joseph McGuinness on the front and the detail that he is a 'Candidate for South Longford, May 1917' election. The back of this card is totally blank. I believe that this was part of the electioneering publicity to get him elected. The title also states Irish Republican Army, 1916, which did not exist in 1916, at least not at the time of the Easter Rising.

Joseph McGuinness was born in 1875 and was not a young man when he joined the I.V. but still fought in the Four Courts Garrison and for this on 2nd May was sentenced to three years penal servitude and was sent to Lewes Prison. Whilst there he was nominated as the Sinn Fein candidate for the South Longford Parliamentary election that was held on Wednesday 9th May 1917 which he won on a recount by 37 votes. To get him elected the famous slogan was coined "Vote Him in to Get Him Out". He was a member of the first Dail and was re-elected in 1921. He supported the Treaty but died on 31st May 1922 and was buried at Glasnevin Cemetery where he was given a funeral with full military honours.

CAPT. R. MONTEITH,

1st Batt. Dublin Regiment, Irish Volunteers.

(Deported under Defence of the Realm Act, 1914)

City Printing Co., Limerick.

Monteith, Captain Robert

Robert Monteith was born at Newtownmountkennedy on 1st March 1879. He joined the British Army in 1895 and served in India and South Africa before being discharged with the rank of bombardier. He returned to Ireland and worked in the Ordnance Department at Island Bridge. In 1913 he joined the Irish Volunteers and after refusing to rejoin the British Army he was dismissed from his job. He eventually went to Limerick as a drill instructor to the I.V. He was seconded to help Casement in Germany and returned with him via a German submarine, landing at Banna Strand. He evaded capture and made his way to the USA where he worked as a foreman at Ford Motors. He died in Detroit on 18th February 1953.

Mulcahy, Richard James

Richard James Mulcahy was born in Waterford on 10th May 1886 and educated locally and at Thurles. In 1913 he was living in Dublin and was a founding member of the I.V. He also joined the Gaelic League and was a member of the I.R.B. At Ashbourne he was second in command and recognised as the military strategist behind its success. For his part in the Rising he was sent to Knutsford and then Frongoch, eventually being released on 24th December 1916. Returning to Dublin he was made Commandant of the Dublin Brigade of the I.V. and in 1918 elected to the first Dail for Dublin-Clontarf and appointed Minister of Defence. In March of the following year he was made Chief of Staff of the I.R.A. Together with Michael Collins he directed the War of Independence against the British forces. He supported the Treaty and was appointed Commander of the army of the Provisional Government during the Civil War. He pushed through the Emergency Powers that led to the execution of 77 anti-Treaty supporters. Elected as T.D. for Dublin-North West in 1921 and 1922 he again held the post of Defence Minster. In 1924 he resigned over the revolt in the army by Civil War officers who he wanted to dismiss. He was back in government in 1927 as the Local Government Minister. His life in Irish politics took many twists and turns. Several times rejected at elections he was elected leader of Fine Gael in 1944. His last government post was as Minister of Education in 1948. He retired from politics in 1961 and died in Dublin on 16th December 1971.

DICK MULCAHY, T.D.

RICHARD O'CARROLL, T.C. (Dublin).
Shot in Action.

O'Carroll, Richard

Richard O'Carroll was a trade unionist and politician. He was secretary of the Incorporated Brick and Stonelayers Union and a friend of James Connolly. In 1906 he was elected to Dublin City Council for the Mansion House ward. In the council he was leader of the Labour Party. He served as an officer in the Irish Volunteers and on Wednesday 26th April he was taken prisoner by a group of soldiers led by Captain Bowen Colthurst. After preliminary interrogation Colthurst shot him in the back and left him in the street. Local citizens loaded him onto a cart and took him to a hospital where he later died.

O'Hanrahan, Michael

Michael O'Hanrahan was born on St. Patrick's Day, 17th March 1877, in New Ross, Co. Wexford, but the family moved to Carlow whilst he was a youth. Here he grew up in a Fenian household. He founded the Workman's Club and a branch of the Gaelic League. Together with his mother and his siblings he moved to Dublin where they lived at 67 Connaught Street, Phibsboro. In 1905 he joined Sinn Fein and for two years was its joint Honorary Secretary. By 1913 he had joined the I.V. and was its Quartermaster General. In 1915 his first novel, *Swordsman of the Brigade*, was published. During the Rising he was second in command to MacDonagh at Jacob's Biscuit Factory. At the surrender he was taken to Richmond Barracks, together with his brother Henry. He was sentenced to death and in the early hours of the morning of 4th May he was seen by his sisters in his tiny cell where watched over by them he made his will. It was witnessed by two British soldiers, Sergeant Major Wright and Lieutenant Barnett. At dawn's first light he was taken from his cell and executed.

O'Hanrahan had two further books published posthumously in 1919: *When the Normans Came* and *Irish Heroines*.

Then let our slogan rouse the world,
Our cries of triumph wake the dead,
When Ireland's foes are downward hurled
And Freedom crowns Her Dear Dark Head

O'Hanrahan, Henry

Henry O'Hanrahan, known as Harry to his family, was a founder member of the I.V. and worked as a clerk in their headquarters. During the Rising he fought with his brother at Jacob's Biscuit Factory. He was sentenced to death on the 6th May 1916 but this was commuted to penal servitude. This photograph may have been taken on St. Patrick's Day as he appears to have a large bunch of shamrock in his coat lapel.

O'Higgins, Kevin Christopher

Kevin Christopher O'Higgins was born in 1892 at Stradbally, Co. Laois. He studied at University College, Dublin gaining a B.A. and was called to the Bar in 1923. He was a member of the I.V. and elected to the first Dail for Laois-Offaly. He was assistant to Cosgrave and a Treaty supporter working with Collins before becoming Minister for Economic Affairs. In 1923 his father was killed in front of his family. He was appointed Minister of Justice in 1924 and was the main author of the Public Safety Act. On 11th July 1927 on his way to mass in Botterstown he was assassinated by Republicans.

HENRY O'HANRAHAN
(Brother of Michael O'Hanrahan, who was Executed),
Sentenced to Penal Servitude.

The late KEVIN O'HIGGINS, Minister for Justice, Irish Free State.

TH: O'RAHILLY.
One of the Leaders, who was Snot in Act on, G.P.O. Area.

O'Rahilly, Michael

Michael O'Rahilly was born in Kerry and worked as a journalist but was also a member of the Gaelic League and Sinn Fein. He spent some time in America and was married there. It was at his request that MacNeill wrote his *The North Began* article. Together with Bulmer Hobson he organised the founding meeting of the Volunteers, became their Director of Arms and helped organise the Howth gun running. After doing MacNeill's bidding to countermand the order to rise on Easter Sunday he returned to Dublin and joined the garrison of the G.P.O. and was later killed during the evacuation of the building.

JOHN O'REILLY
(Irish Republican Army).
Killed in Action at City Hall, Dublin,
Easter Monday, 1916.

O'Reilly, John

This sub-caption of *Irish Republican Army* is somewhat misleading as the I.R.A. only came into being after the Easter Rising. O'Reilly as the caption states, was killed at City Hall. He held the rank of lieutenant of the Citizen Army. He may have been the J. O'Reilly employed by Dublin Corporation as a water inspector in 1906.

Photo] [Keogh Bros.
JAMES O'SULLIVAN.

O'Sullivan, James

James O'Sullivan, seen here in his I.V. uniform, was an active member of the Limerick Volunteers. For his part in the Rising he was sentenced to five years penal servitude. He was a personal friend of the Daly family and bears a striking resemblance to Edward Daly.

Pearse, Patrick Henry

Patrick Pearse was the mouthpiece of the rebellion. His famous speech "the fools, the fools, the fools" at the funeral of Jermiah O'Donovan Rossa set him apart from his contempories. Born into a family of four sisters and a brother he had an English father and an Irish mother. The family ran a stone masonry business. From his youth, Pearse had visions of an independent Ireland, believing "Bloodshed is a cleansing and sanctifying thing". The Easter Rising would fit in well with Christ and the crucifixion and the spilling of Irish blood to achieve his "mystic" imaginations.

Pearse passed the bar exam but never practised. Instead he founded his bi-lingual school, St. Enda's at Ranelagh. A prominent member of the Gaelic League, he wrote articles for *Irish Freedom*, a paper that was financed by the I.R.B. of which he soon became a member and then swiftly a member of their military council. He was a founder member of the Irish Volunteers and played a significant part in the planning of the Rising. As president of the newly formed Irish Republic and commander in chief of the Republican Army he surrendered to General Lowe "In order to prevent the further slaughter of Dublin citizens".

IRISH REBELLION, MAY 1916

P. H. PEARSE.
Commandant-General of the Army of the Irish Republic),
Executed May 3rd, 1916.
One of the signatories of the "Irish Republic Proclamation."

WILLIAM PEARSE
(Younger Brother of P. H. Pearse, also Executed).
Executed at Kilmainham Prison, May 4th, 1916.

Pearse, William

Patrick's younger brother Willie worked as a sculptor in the family-run memorial masonry business and was a part-time actor. He was a founder member of the Volunteers, worked in their headquarters, assisted in the running of St. Enda's and was his brother's aide-de-camp in the G.P.O. during the Rising.

GEORGE NOBLE COUNT PLUNKETT, F.S.A.
(Father of Joseph Plunkett, who was Executed, and of George and John Plunkett, Sentenced to Penal Servitude),
Arrested May 1st, 1916, and detained in Richmond Barracks till June 5th, and now Deported to Oxford.

Plunkett, Count George

Count Plunkett was a descendant of Saint Oliver Plunkett, a Papal count and a director of the National Museum. Prior to the Rising the Plunkett family home at Kimmage was turned into an I.R.B. training camp, where many like Michael Collins stayed in a mill on the family farm at Larkhill making bombs, pikes and bayonets to pass the time of day. The men who stayed there became known as the Kimmage Garrison and were led by George Plunkett. Collins was made Joseph Plunkett's aide-de camp as a result of his contact with him at Kimmage. The plans for the Rising had now been in place for several months.

The Plunkett family took an active part in the Rising – his niece Philomena (Mimi) acted as a secret transatlantic courier.

JOSEPH PLUNKETT (son of Count Plunkett),
Commandant-General Irish Republican Army,
Executed May 4th, 1916.
Who was married a few hours before his execution.

Plunkett, Joseph

Joseph Mary Plunkett was a poet, writer and Director of Operations for the I.V. making him the architect of the plans for the Rising. Sickly both as a child and in adulthood, much of his life was spent in the warmth of Sicily. A member of both the I.R.B. and the I.V. he travelled to Germany to seek help for the Rising but his effete appearance did not impress the Germans. He was due to be married on Easter Sunday to Grace Gifford but instead turned out for the Rising, his throat swathed in bandages from a recent operation. After being sentenced to death, he married Gifford the night before his execution in the chapel at Kilmainham.

J. E. REDMOND, M.P.

PHOTO BY
ELLIOTT & FRY,
LONDON.

Redmond, John Edward

The Redmond family of Wexford were steeped in politics when John Edward was born on 1st September 1856 at Ballytret House. At Westminster in 1876 he was assistant to his father and soon became a firm Parnellite. He was elected unopposed for New Ross in 1881 but was ejected from the Commons on the day of his maiden speech. In 1888 he was sentenced to five weeks hard labour for an inflammatory speech. After Parnell's death the two factions of the Irish Parliamentary Party reunited and elected Redmond as their leader, but it was the election of 1912 that gave the I.P.P. the balance of power allowing Redmond to exchange support for the Asquith government for a promise of Home Rule which was eventually achieved on 18th September 1914. Redmond died of a heart attack in London on 6th March 1918.

Savage, Martin

Martin Savage was born in Streamstown, Co. Sligo into a Fenian family in 1898. In 1915 he moved to Dublin where he worked as a grocer. He joined the I.V. and fought in the G.P.O. during the Rising. On his release from Knutsford Prison in 1917 he was appointed lieutenant of 2nd battalion Dublin Brigade. On 19th December 1919 he took part in a failed assassination attempt on Lord French, the Lord Lieutenant of Ireland at Ashtown. During the attempt Savage was shot in the throat and died. After an inquest his body was returned to his family and taken by train to Sligo where crowds turned out to meet his body. He was buried with full military honours in his native town.

This postcard of Savage is the most common known of him. It is full of Irish symbols: the harp, the wolfhound and the Irish Tricolour. The legend printed on the ribbon translates as God Have Mercy on their Souls.

LIEUT. M. SAVAGE,
DIED FOR IRELAND DEC., 19TH 1919.

FRANCIS SHEEHY SKEFFINGTON, M.A.,
Arrested on Easter Monday, and shot without trial at Portobello Barracks, 26th April, 1916.

Skeffington, Francis Sheehy

The pacifist and humanist Francis Skeffington was born on 23rd December 1878 at Bailieborough, Co. Cavan. He was educated at University College, Dublin where he served as registrar for two years. He co-founded the newspaper *Irish Citizen* and served on the Peace Committee during the Lock Out. For a while he was vice-chairman of the Citizen Army and was imprisoned for campaigning against recruitment. He was illegally arrested by Captain Bowen-Colthurst on Tuesday 25th April and taken to Portobello Barracks where the following morning he was executed. His wife, Hanna, was offered £10,000 compensation by the British Government which she refused.

AUSTIN STACK
(Arrested in connection with the Casement landing in Kerry on Good Friday),
Sentenced to Penal Servitude for Life.
COPYRIGHT]

Stack, Austin

Austin Stack was born and bred in his native Kerry and captained the county Gaelic football team in the winning final of 1904. A local taxman, he was a founder member of the Kerry Volunteers and a member of the I.R.B. It was his inability to get Casement released from the police barracks in Tralee that led to him being ostracised by the other Kerry Volunteers during their subsequent imprisonment. Stack claimed he was obeying Dublin orders not to fire a shot until the Rising had begun. He later became Minister for Home Affairs in the Dail from 1920 and an anti-Treaty supporter for which he was jailed in Kilmainham. There, in 1924, he went on a hunger strike for 41 days. He died in Dublin on 27th April 1929.

Capt. THOMAS WAFER
("C." Co., 2nd Batt.)
Killed in the Hibernian Bank,
April 26th, 1916.

Wafer, Thomas Joseph

Thomas Joseph Wafer, whose name is often spelt Weafer, was an Enniscorthy man who moved to north Dublin with his wife and set up a cabinet making business. Aged 26 he held the rank of captain in the 2nd Battalion, Dublin Brigade and was killed whilst fighting in the Hibernian Bank at the corner of Lower Abbey Street and Sackville Street. His body was burnt in the building.

Chapter 7: Revolutionary Priests

The Catholic Church in Ireland around 1916 preferred the status quo, no surprises, no shocks. They helped maintain law and order by their conformity and consistency. It suited the church and it also suited the British administration who "encouraged" them to do so. This position was maintained by the vast majority of the clergy who toed the Rome or rather Armagh (the principal seat of the R.C. Church in Ireland) line. No other institution in the land had such a platform or passionate orators in the form of the pulpit and the priest. The formation and rise of Nationalist movements like the Gaelic League and the Gaelic Athletic Association were acceptable, as they kept traditions that the church condoned, but the rapid growth of Sinn Fein alarmed the bishops. Whilst most of the members of Sinn Fein attended mass and communion during and after the Rising none the less the clergy would have to keep an eye on them. The bishops saw Sinn Fein as a threat to their position, both locally and nationally. So from the pulpit came the message both implied and explicit that whilst fighting for the Faith was acceptable, fighting for control of one's country was acceptable only with the bishop's blessing. In the main, providing a priest did not overstep the line with his Republican/Nationalist views, he was allowed to remain in his post.

In Tang, near Ballymahon, the parish priest Father O'Reilly held very Nationalist views. He started a popular branch of the Gaelic League and later established an I.V. brigade for which he secured some of the Howth rifles. Father O'Reilly had overstepped the mark and was removed from his parish by the combined pressure of his bishop and Dublin Castle. Another priest, Father Clarke, spoke out against conscription at a meeting in Ballymore saying "Who ever is with us is here today those who are not are against us". This did not go down well with the R.I.C. constables who attended the meeting. However, these local clergy were few and far between and it was left to several high profile priests who were unafraid to air their thoughts on a more national stage. One such man was Father Michael O'Flannagan who earned the sobriquet "The Sinn Fein Priest". O'Flannagan was in attendance at the major Republican gatherings and not because he was performing his calling. At the O'Donovan Rossa funeral he can be seen next to Pearse when he made his famous speech "The fools, the fools, the fools".

Staṅley-   22 Westmoreland St, Dublin.
Mícheál o'Flannagáin
Máṅta 1919.

Michael O'Flannagan

O'Flannagan was born near Castlerea, Co. Roscommon in 1876 and was educated at the local national school, Summerhill School and at Maynooth where in 1900 he was ordained. He was sent to America on a fund-raising tour from which he did not return until 1907. He returned to Summerhill where he taught until 1912 and then spent two years as a curate in Co. Roscommon where he became deeply involved in land agitation. From here he went to Clifoney, Co. Sligo and finally to Dublin where during the Rising he was part of the G.P.O. garrison. His first political involvement came when he campaigned for Count Plunkett at the by-election of 1917. On 25th October 1917 he was elected vice-president of Sinn Fein and began an anti-Conscription campaign. In June the following year he was suspended from his duties by his bishop for recruiting priests to join Sinn Fein. During the War of Independence he served as a Dail judge and became an anti-Treaty supporter. In 1926, at the Sinn Fein Ard Fheis, it was his influence that defeated de Valera's proposal to ban the Oath of Allegiance. O'Flannagan blamed de Valera for splitting Republicans when he formed his party Fianna Fail. Disillusioned by these politics he resigned from Sinn Fein though he remained a supporter. Finally silenced by his bishop his Republican views did not stop him from supporting the Irish Brigade that went to Spain to fight Franco. In 1937 he was touring America again but when he returned he settled to editing the letters of John O'Donovan. Canon O' Flannagan died in Dublin on 7th August 1942 and is buried in Glasnevin.

Edward Thomas O'Dwyer

"Ireland will never be content as a province. God made her a nation. and while grass grows and water runs there will be men in Ireland to dare and die for her."
(Extract from speech of the Most Rev Dr. O'Dwyer when the freedom of Limerick City was conferred on him, Sept. 14th, 1916).

This postcard commemorates the freedom bestowed on O'Dwyer by the City of Limerick as the text in the panel on the left is an extract from his speech of thanks.

The west of Ireland and Limerick in particular had long been a Republican stronghold. At the time of the Rising there was a mixture of both sacred and secular. John Daly, the old Fenian, was a powerful voice in the city's chambers whilst across the city in Park House, Corbally, a bishop who was unafraid to speak his mind despite what his brother bishops might say or think was Edward Thomas O'Dwyer.

Edward Thomas O'Dwyer was born at Lattin, Co. Tipperary on 22nd January 1842. The family moved to Limerick where he was educated locally before he was ordained at Maynooth in 1867. He was appointed curate of St. Michael's Parish, Limerick, then in June 1886 he was consecrated Bishop of Limerick. He opposed land agitation and was critical of the Irish Parliamentary Party. Unlike other bishops he refused to sign the condemnation of Charles Stewart Parnell. O'Dwyer attacked Redmond for his pro-British stance and advocated that Ireland should be neutral in the First World War. When, in 1915 a group of Irish workers were attacked in Liverpool he wrote eloquently to the newspapers stating "Their crime is that they are not ready to die for England. Why should they? What have they or their fore-bearers ever got from England that they should die for her". Nationalists seized on his words and reproduced them in pamphlet and postcard form. This free-thinking man was the first member of the hierarchy to defend the men of the Easter Rising. When requested by General Maxwell to discipline two of his clergy (Fathers Hall and Bayes) for their Nationalist preaching he turned on Maxwell, condemning him for his actions in the execution of the leader of the Rising and the deportation of thousands of others and accusing his regime as being "one of the worst and blackest chapters in the history of the misgovernment of the country". Such was his response to Maxwell that support from the length and breadth of the country was showered on him. On 14th September 1916 he was given the Freedom of the City of Limerick, a freedom that was short-lived as five days later on Saturday 19th August 1917 he died there.

Archbishop Daniel Mannix

An tAtair ró-oirmitoneaċ Domnall ua Mainċín, Ollaṁ Diaċta, Ároeaṙboᵹ Melbouṙn.

Archbishop Daniel Mannix of Melbourne, Australia was another cleric whose views were to earn him a reputation that set him apart. Mannix was born on 4th March 1864 in Charlieville, Co. Cork and was educated locally before being ordained at Maynooth in 1890 where he finally rose to become President of the College in 1903, a post he held until 1912. He was made co-adjutor Bishop of Melbourne which was at that time a strongly Irish Catholic centre. He denounced the First World War and spoke out against Conscription, views that made him persona non grata in the city. In 1917 he was consecrated archbishop, a post he held for 47 years. Though he spoke against the Rising he led the cortege of Terence MacSwiney through the streets of London. His Nationalist views were evident in his virulent criticism of the Black and Tans and the tactics of the Auxiliaries. In 1920 he received the Freedom of the City of New York. From here his intention was to sail to Ireland, but on 8th August the R.M.S. *Baltic* was stopped en route and Mannix was arrested by the British authorities and taken to Penzance, Cornwall. Stopped from his Nationalist speaking tour of Ireland he none the less held night time gatherings in England and Scotland. Back in Melbourne he founded the Irish Relief Fund to support the families of those who had been shot or were in prison for fighting for the cause of Irish independence. This controversial man, an advocate of non-violence, died on 6th November 1963 and is buried in the crypt of St. Patrick's Cathedral, Melbourne.

This portrait, attributed to Lafayette, shows Mannix in his robes as Archbishop. The caption is totally printed in Gaelic and translates as The Very Reverend Father Daniel Mannix, Professor of Divinity, Archbishop of Melbourne.

Other Clergy

In Dublin at the time of the Rising was a man who was considered not only an intellectual but also the greatest bishop of Dublin. William Joseph Walsh was born at Essex Quay, Dublin on 30th January 1841. He was ordained at Maynooth in 1866 where his academic ability was recognised and in 1880 he was made President of the College, a post he held until his appointment as Bishop of Dublin on 3rd July 1885. His appointment was opposed by the government because of his known support of the Land League and his strong Nationalist leanings. It was said that these leanings prevented him from receiving a cardinal's hat. He lost faith in the I.P.P. in 1917, becoming a supporter of Sinn Fein, and was strongly opposed to the bill that partitioned Ireland. His learned writings were on subjects many and various. He died in Dublin on 9th April 1921, his coffin draped in the Irish Tricolour.

Franciscan friars of the Capuchin order, who may not have espoused the cause for which the Republicans died, after the Rising comforted the executed and their families. These men from St. Mary of the Angels, Church Street, Dublin were Father Aloysuis, Father Augustine, Father Albert and Father Columbus. The clergy's attitude to the Rising changed as quickly as that of the general population. It did not want to seem to be out of step, by being in step they could once again enjoy the support of the people of Ireland.

Chapter 8: Ruins

Postcards of the Easter Rising mainly fall into two categories: portraits of the personalities involved in it and scenes of destruction and devastation. This chapter is devoted to the latter. The scenes mainly show the effect of the British artillery, both field and naval, though the destruction of Sackville Street in the early part of the Rising was caused not by artillery but by the drunken behaviour of the Dublin slum dwellers. Those from the slums, considered to be the worst in Europe at the time, could not believe their luck. The best that Ireland had to offer was theirs for the taking and it was all free of charge. The looting led to fires that swept the street and what the slum dwellers started the British guns continued.

The postcards shown are just a sample of those issued by publishers large and small and by the same token show a small sample of the devastation caused. It is said "a picture paints a thousand words". Therefore the postcards shown will need little explanation.

East side of Sackville Street from O'Connell's Bridge. The building in the centre was the D.B.C.   W. & G. BAIRD, LTD., BELFAS

The building in the centre of this view is all that remains of the D.B.C. (Dublin Bread Company). The centre of the city has been considerably cleared of rubble. Behind the D.B.C can be seen the square ruins of the Hibernian Bank.

Ruins of G.P.O., Dublin.   W. & G. BAIRD, LTD., BELFAST.

Dublin citizens wander about aimlessly taking in their devastated city and the G.P.O. which is little more than a shell. Every publisher produced a view of the G.P.O. This is Baird's offering.

6719—10   THE SINN FEIN REVOLT IN DUBLIN.   ROTARY PHOTO, E.C.
                       GENERAL VIEW OF THE DEVASTATED CITY

Further proof of the disastrous state of Dublin, caused in the main by the wayward shelling of the city.

Just one of the Valentine's Popular "Before and After" series of Postcards.

SINN FEIN REBELLION

CORNER OF SACKVILLE STREET, DUBLIN.   BEFORE AND   ᴇR

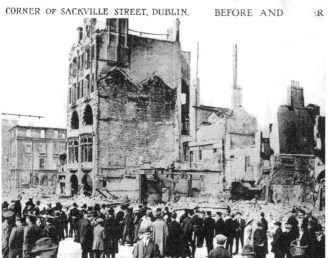

This corner building was colloquially known as Kelly's Fort during the Rising, not only because of its position but because of the sign saying "Gunpowder Office". The sign on another part of the corner states Chancellor Photographer to the King. Chancellor produced photographs of the Rising but to my knowledge none were issued as postcards.

After the Insurrection.—
Corner of Bachelor's Walk and Lr. Sackville Street
which commanded O'Connell Bridge.

Compared to the building next to it Liberty Hall is reasonably intact. James Connolly's headquarters was none the less the target for H.M.S. *Helga* that eventually found its mark.

This is the best and only authentic night time photograph of the Rising, with silhouettes of Parnell's and Nelson's Monuments set against the flames and the night sky.

Irish Rebellion - May 1916.
The wreck they made of Church Street, Dublin.

Amidst all the rubble the children seem to be more interested in the photographer. The caption is misleading because the word "they" perhaps implies that it was the Rebels who caused the damage.

Irish Rebellion, May., 1916.
Henry Street, Dublin, after the shelling of the Rebels.

The citizens climb over the rubble that once was a building with the shell of the post office to the right of this view.

Hotel Metropole, Sackville Street, after the Fire.   [Keogh Bros.

The "Fire" was caused by British shells missing their intended target, the G.P.O.

"The Liberator" stands undamaged whilst all around is destruction.

Sackville Street opposite G.P.O., showing all that is standing of the Imperial Hotel and
Messrs. Clery's Drapery Establishment.

The facade of this building at 22-27 Lower Sackville Street looks precarious. It was subsequently
rebuilt.

After the Insurrection.—Sackville Street. The D.B.C., a picturesque ruin.

This view shows the fate of the D.B.C., devastated but still standing due to its steel frame.

After the Insurrection.—Interior General Post Office, Dublin.

The figures of two soldiers can be seen picking their way through what is left of the building. In the foreground is the twisted remains of a bicycle.

After the Insurrection.—Burning ruins in Upper Sackville Street.

Bemused Dubliners stand and watch the burning ruins at the corner of Cathedral Street.

After the Insurrection.—Ruins of the Hibernian Bank and Lower Abbey Street.

Like the G.P.O., all that remains is the shell of the building. The bank was the last resting place of Thomas Wafer.

Sinn Fein Rebellion, 1916.
Hotel Metropole and
Post Office, Dublin.

Whilst the walls of the G.P.O. are intact that is all of the building that stands. From its roof the "Irish Republic" flagpole hangs precariously. Only the Metropole's side wall still stands.

In the thick of it the *Freeman's Journal* offices stood no chance.

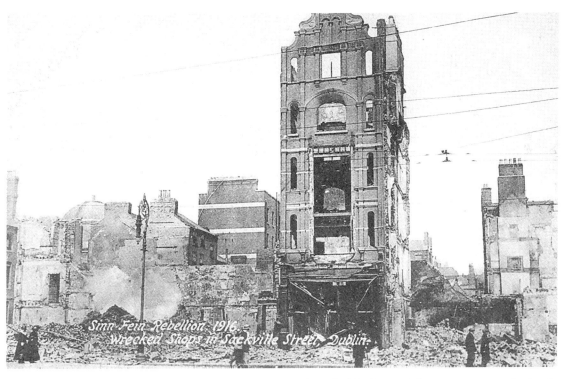

This single standing building is on the east side of Sackville Street. The message on the back of this card reads: "Just another P.C. of Dublin this was once all big shops as high as the … building that is now standing alone".

Corner of Abbey Street, Dublin

This view is just another of utter distruction. The caption is unusual in that it has no mention of Sinn Fein or the Rebellion.

Ruins at Dublin from top of Nelson's Pillar

The view from the top of the Pillar shows buildings without roofs and in the distance the Customs House.

Ruins of North Earl Street, Dublin.

This view shows the devastating results of the Rising, the G.P.O. without a roof and all other buildings in the same state. These Valentine's views with the caption "Ruins of" are the photographic work of Lieutenant Sol Archer whose address in 1916 was the United Services Club, Dublin.

Ruins of North Street, Dublin. This view from the Pillar is no different from any other as all that can be seen is destruction.

Ruins of G.P.O., Dublin, as seen from top of Nelson's Pillar

Corner of Middle Abbey St, & O'Connell St. Dublin. After "The Sinn Fein Rising."

Unlike other views Dubliners seem to be going about their business rather than looking at the ruins, enabled to do so by the cleared streets.

Skeleton of Clery's and Imperial Hotel O'Connell St. Dublin. After "The Sinn Fein Rising."

The caption is exactly right – all that is left is the skeleton of Clery's.

The Hibernian Bank, O'Connell Street, Dublin.
After "The Sinn Fein Rising."

This building was sited at 12 and 13 O'Connell Street.

Portion of Bolton Street, Dublin.
from The Sinn Fein Rising.

This nondescript pile of rubble with the shell of a derelict building in the background is in Bolton Street.

Being sited at 43, Sackville Street the Y.M.C.A. was right in the thick of the fighting. It would appear that a temporary canopy has been constructed over the entrance to fend off any falling masonry.

In the distance the sky can be seen through the windowless G.P.O. Nelson's Pillar takes up the central part of the view and a heavily scaffolded building that appears ready to collapse is to the left.

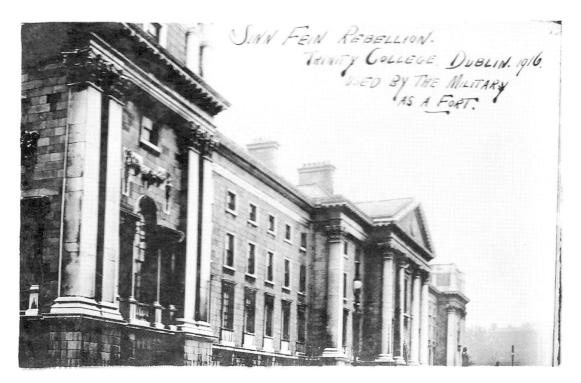

The caption says it all. Trinity College was part of Plunkett's plan to take control of the city. Lack of manpower meant this had to be abandoned. Initially students and a hotchpotch of soldiers on leave took control of the College until they were replaced by regular soldiers.

Another view of Abbey Street that being so central suffered severely. None the less life goes on for most and those who "have time to stand and stare".

Time has now passed and Sackville Street has been cleared of rubble. The photographer has focused in on the curved corner building of the Dublin United Tramways Co.

The remains of the shops on the west side of Sackville Street with the ruins of the Hotel Metropole in the background.

The shelter has an advertising sign across the top stating "Branch of the Dublin Coffee Palace Hotel 6 Townsend St." Townsend Street is a continuation of D'Olier Street.

This location is identified by the sign over the first building next to the ruins which says Wynn's, referring to Wynn's Hotel, which was at 35-39 Lower Abbey Street and an establishment that had been in existence since 1845.

Interior View Ruins of Coliseum Theatre, Dublin.

The theatre was sited at 24 Henry Street and opened its doors to the public on 5th April 1915. It was never rebuilt.

Henry Street, Dublin, showing side of G.P.O. after the bombardment.

Whilst the street has been cleared for traffic or pedestrians should they need it, all around is rubble. Just above the head of the two men is the canopy to the entrance of the Coliseum Theatre. Higher still is a sign for MacInerney at 26/28 Henry Street who were "General Drapers and Gentlemen's Outfitters" and above all of these the dome of Arnotts.

Chapter 9: The Postal Service after the Rising

With the surrender life slowly returned to some form of normality. The Rising had caused great problems for the citizens of Dublin and everywhere there were shortages. This was just as true of the postal service.

Lord Wimborne, the Lord Lieutenant of Ireland, who after the Rising was exonerated of any blame over the Rebellion, had pressed for action to be taken both before and during the Easter week. Before he had urged that the "Sinn Feiners" should be arrested. During the Rising he pressured A.H. Norway, Secretary of the Post Office, to resume delivery of the mail. Norway, aware of the danger that might befall the appearance of his men in uniform on the streets of Dublin refused and Wimborne reluctantly conceded.

Mail did start to move again when a small consignment was shipped off to England on Saturday 29th April, but aware that there was still a tension in Dublin, Norway refused again to restart the service without reasonable assurances from the Army that his postmen would be safe. Satisfied with the Army's response he ordered the resumption of deliveries which began on Wednesday 3rd May. Though post boxes had not been emptied there was still a backlog of mail waiting in the offices in and around Dublin to be delivered and even more waiting to come into the city from the rest of the country to be sorted and delivered.

Whatever mail there was in the G.P.O. was by now no more than grey, silken crumbling fragments of letters and parcels that had gone up in flames with the building. Thousands of letters were lost in the building that was still smouldering days after the Rising had ended. It was not only the mail that was lost in the inferno but the equipment to cancel, sort, distribute and deliver it. It was left to the ingenuity of the postal workers to adapt any form of equipment to hand to make up for these shortages in their efforts to get the mail moving again.

Put into action for cancellation is a parcel roller from the Dublin office. All that is visible of this cancellation is "Dublin Office". What the cancellation should show is Dublin Parcel Office.

111

This Valentine postcard was sent to "Bridge End, Belfast". The halfpenny stamp on this postcard has been cancelled by what appears to be a smudged shape of a Maltese Cross, a shape which had been formerly used to cancel stamps in the 19th century. To my knowledge this cancellation is not recorded but in times such as these any form of cancellation would have been put to use to keep the mail moving.

When it was safe to enter the G.P.O. building £185 was found intact but it was estimated that £2,792 18s 2d of official money was lost due to the conflict which included £149 10s that was found on one of the members of the G.P.O. garrison when he was arrested.

New premises had to be found to restart the postal service and by Wednesday 3rd May an improvised sorting office made up of all sorts of different size benches, tables and desks was set up in the Rotunda. The Amiens Street Parcels Office helped fill the void by taking up some of the duties that would have been performed by the Sackville Street office, but above all it was the staff that went the extra mile and worked tirelessly to put the postal service back on its feet. This was recognised by Norway, who returned to the head office in London in 1917 and who bore the responsibility for and the achievement of getting the service running again. He graciously paid tribute to his untiring staff. "… My staff as a whole did their work out of self-respect. But I think a little extra leave would be much appreciated".

As post offices began opening they were swamped by pensioners and separation wives, whose husbands were fighting for the British Army in the First World War, to collect their pay. Soldiers were sent to control the crowds who were at their wits end for money to feed their starving families. Fearful that large amounts of money on the move might be a target Norway insisted that the movement of money from the Bank of Ireland to the various post offices should be accompanied by an armoured vehicle of the sort used during the Rising.

The General Post Office in Sackville Street, which during the Rising was the insurgents' headquarters, is a magnificent building, second only to the Customs House in Dublin. It was designed by an Armagh man, Francis Johnston (1760–1829), who was responsible for the design of many of Dublin's fine buildings and it stands on what was originally the site of a barracks. The main Dublin post office had previously had many sites, most notably College Green which ceased in this role with the opening of the Sackville Street building in 1818. The foundation stone was laid on 12th August 1814 by the Lord Lieutenant of Ireland, Charles Whitworth, 1st Earl of Whitworth. The cost of the three storey building was £50,000. Sackville Street G.P.O. opened its doors to the public on the feast of the Epiphany, 6th January 1818. The building befits its site, measuring 223ft in width, 50ft tall and has a depth of 150ft. The commanding portico is 50ft in length and comprises six Ionic columns which support a pediment that acts as a plinth for three statues. The triangular shape of the pediment originally held a relief of the Royal Coat of Arms which was removed at the time of the restoration of the building The three statues depict the mythical figures of Hibernian in the centre, Fidelity to the left and Mercury to the right, all three being the work of John Smyth. The portico is of Portland stone whilst the main building is of granite. At the time of the Rising the building had just been renovated at great cost. By the time of the surrender all that remained of it was a charred smouldering shell. Its future was now in the balance and there was much discussion over the options, one of which was that with the expected passing of the Home Rule Bill and Independence it should become the Irish House of Parliament. It was not until 11th July 1926 that it was restored to its former glory when, after an extensive renovation, it was opened by the Taoiseach, Mr. W.T. Cosgrove.

Today the building is a shrine to Irish Independence. Displayed on one of the interior walls is a plaque written in Gaelic and English commemorating the Easter Rising. In the entrance stands a bronze statue of Cuchulainn, the mythical Irish hero, by Oliver Sheppard. On the outside of the building is a simple plaque that states Ard Oifig An Phuist, The General Post Office.

This postcard of the G.P.O. shows the building and the street at the turn of the century with open-top trams advertising food stuffs some of which, like Jacob's biscuits are still available today. The Union Jack can be seen flying from the Prince's Street corner.

Chapter 10: War of Independence

It is perhaps surprising that despite all that has been said about postcards there were few issued on what was arguably the most important event of this decade in Irish history, namely the War of Independence. The Easter Rising postcards were permitted, I believe, because the British authorities were fearful of antagonising public opinion further. In the case of the War of Independence the "gloves were off" and the British Government were not going to allow anything that might further glorify the Nationalists' aspirations for an Irish Republic. It is therefore likely that few, if any, postcards were published on the subject and by the same token publishers were afraid of reprisal by the British Authorities if they did publish.

Kevin Barry

KEVIN BARRY.

This is the most common portrait of Barry, seen in his rugby jersey.

One noticeable exception to the above was the execution of young Kevin Barry. The Irish have a strong oral tradition and today Barry is still celebrated in verse almost to the extent as the day when he was hanged.

Kevin Barry was born in Dublin on 20th January 1902. At the age of six his father died and his mother moved the family of six to her family's home in Co. Carlow. Barry attended St. Mary's College, Rathmines where he played for the junior rugby team. In 1919 he won a scholarship to study medicine at U.C.D. and joined the I.V. He was an active member of the I.R.A. and at the age of sixteen took part in several raids, including a successful one on the King's Inn, the controlling body of Irish barristers where a sizeable arms cache was seized.

On 20th September 1920 he joined up with other I.R.A. members in Bolton Street, their plan to ambush a British Army truck collecting bread from Monk's Bakery in Church Street and "relieve" the soldiers of their weapons. Barry was stationed at the back of the truck with a .38 Mauser. When challenged, the soldiers quickly laid down their weapons, but suddenly a shot rang out. The startled attackers started firing. Barry's gun jammed and he dived for cover under the truck as the rest of the gang fled, but he was soon spotted and arrested. One British soldier was dead and two others died later of their severe wounds.

Barry was taken to the South Dublin Union where he was interrogated and tortured. At 10 o'clock on 20th October Barry's court martial was due to begin, but he did not enter the court until about 10.25 as the vehicle bringing him to the trial broke down. He was charged with murder and his only comment was that he did not accept the jurisdiction of the court. The court martial convicted him of the murder of Private Whitehead on the grounds that he was one of the members of the ambush party that committed the murder and was therefore equally guilty. Private Whitehead had been killed by a .45 calibre bullet but Barry's Mauser fired a .38 bullet, so it was not his gun that had killed Private Whitehead.

The trial over, Barry was returned to Mountjoy Prison where that night he learnt of his fate, that he was to be hanged on 1st November. There was an international outcry over the sentence, including a plea for leniency from the Vatican in particular because he was only 18 years old. The evening before his execution he was visited by his mother and his brothers and sisters. He was hanged the following morning and his body buried in a plot by the women's prison. On 14th October 2001 his remains were exhumed and along with nine other Nationalists his body was interred at Glasnevin after a state funeral.

Much was made of Barry's age when he was hanged, but it should also be noted that the three British soldiers who died were Private Marshall Whitehead aged 20 years, Private Thomas Humphries aged 19 years and Private Harold Washington believed to be aged 15 years.

Though the Kevin Barry episode became a cause celebre, the Irish War of Independence was littered with actions that were a credit to neither side. The I.R.A. fought a guerrilla war where they would "hit and run" a British force which then retaliated with harsh indiscriminate acts in an effort to intimidate the populace at large. The British authorities used the Black and Tans and later the Auxiliaries to fight their battles for them. These two groups were well-paid mercenaries from the ranks of the British Army who were encouraged to take the law unto themselves in an effort to defeat the I.R.A.

The War of Independence began on 21st January 1919 when a group of men from 3rd Tipperary Brigade led by Sean Tracy and Dan Breen attacked and killed two R.I.C. constables escorting a shipment of dynamite at Soloheadbeg, Co. Tipperary. Thereafter the I.R.A. attacked banks, barracks, post offices, tax offices and the R.I.C. themselves. On 14th February 1920 a brigade of 120 men, led by Ernie O'Malley and Eion O'Duffy, destroyed the R.I.C. barracks at Ballytrain, Co. Monaghan.

In Midletown, Co. Cork on 5th June a group of Cameron Highlanders were ambushed and their weapons taken from them. As a reprisal later that day the Highlanders attacked the town. The towns of Lahinch, Milton Malbray and Ennistymon were burnt by troops on 22nd September 1920 after six R.I.C. constables had been killed in an ambush earlier that day.

The litany was always the same: attack followed by reprisal, reprisal against innocent citizens that only alienated them further. These actions happened time and again mainly in the south and west of the country though no area was immune. This cost the lives of many from both sides but there was also a great financial cost to cities, towns, and businesses.

The most notorious incident of the war was the actions of Sunday 21st November, forever known as Bloody Sunday. In the early morning of that day eleven British Intelligence agents were killed on Michael Collins' instructions by his intelligence unit known as "the Squad". As a reprisal the Black and Tans fired into the crowds at a Dublin versus Tipperary Gaelic football match killing twelve and wounding 60 or more. There were more killings to follow for that evening Peadar Clancy, Dick McKee and Conor Clune were "shot while trying to escape" from Dublin Castle.

When on 11th December the city centre of Cork was burnt and looted by the Black and Tans and Auxiliaries the cost amounted to about £3,000,000 in money of the day and left the city in ruins. The then Chief Secretary for Ireland, Sir Hamar Greenwood, proclaimed that the city was set on fire by the I.R.A.

After Cork Fire, Dec. 1920. Patrick Street.

The small town of Balbriggan was almost destroyed when 54 houses, a hosiery factory and four public houses were destroyed on 21st September 1920 by the Black and Tans.

In an effort to bring the British authorities to their knees de Valera sanctioned an attack on the Customs House in Dublin. On 25th May 1921 at approximately 1 o'clock over a hundred I.R.A. men attacked the building and set it alight with paraffin. The Auxiliaries were alerted of the attack and soon arrived and for 30 minutes a firefight ensued. With the building ablaze many I.R.A. men left with their hands raised in surrender.

The result of the raid was several civilians and five I.R.A. members dead and many more wounded; 80 I.R.A. men were taken prisoner. The building was devastated, its dome crashing down into its structure. As a propaganda coup it had the desired effect, but for the I.R.A. the loss of so many men was catastrophic. This action alone did not bring the war to an end but it and the other attacks focused the British Government to enter into peace negotiations with the Irish Nationalists.

Though the fighting with the British was ostensibly over the struggle for independence would take another year before it was achieved, and it wasn't until Easter Monday 1949 that the Republic of Ireland was formally declared, fulfilling the aspirations of the hardline Nationalists.

Patrick Street after Cork Fire, December, 1920.

An artist's impression of the burning Customs House.

Chapter 11: Treaty Conference

Throughout the country there was a voluble sigh of relief when on 11th July 1921 a truce was announced that bought to a close the bitterly fought, vicious and violent Irish War of Independence.

IRISH PEACE CONFERENCE, JULY, 1921.
Truce Day, July 11th, 1921.

Previous to this talks had been going on as delegations from both sides sought to find a solution to end the fighting. On Friday 8th July General Neville Macready met with the I.R.A. leaders at the Mansion House in Dublin. The general was roundly criticised when a photograph of him being greeted by the Lord Mayor of Dublin Laurence O'Neill showed he had an automatic pistol in the right hand pocket of his uniform.

After three long years the fighting was over to all extents. According to Collins the I.R.A. had only weeks of fighting in them and were desperately short of men, money and ammunition. As for the British the war was costing them in men, money and international reputation. Their tactics in trying to overcome the I.R.A. had alienated the country, Ulster apart, and they were fighting a losing battle despite the plight of the enemy.

IRISH PEACE CONFERENCE, JULY, 1921.   Delegates leaving Dun Laoghaire.
E. & S Ltd., Dublin]   [Photo, Hogan, Dublin.

The day after the signing of the truce de Valera left Dun Laoghaire with a delegation for London. Seen here is that delegation who are from left to right Arthur Griffith, Robert Barton, Eamon de Valera, Count Plunkett and Laurence O'Neil, the Lord Mayor of Dublin.

With the news that talks on a truce were taking place at the Mansion House crowds of Dubliners gathered there to catch a glimpse of their leaders but also to lend moral support to the discussions. The day following the signing an Irish delegation led by de Valera as President of Dail Eireann together with Arthur Griffith, Austin Stack, Erskine Childers, Robert Barton and Count Plunkett boarded the Irish ferry at Kingstown.

Three days later they were in 10 Downing Street, London discussing the terms of the treaty with the British Prime Minister David Lloyd George. De Valera returned to Dublin to seek ratification from the Dail. On 24th August he informed Lloyd George that the terms had been rejected with the full backing of the Dail.

IRISH PEACE CONFERENCE, JULY, 1921.   General Macready entering Mansion House with Lord Mayor.
E. & S. Ltd., Dublin]   [Photo, Hogan, Dublin

ARTHUR GRIFFITH, T.D., and EAMON DE VALERA, T.D.,
at the Mansion House Peace Conference, 4th July, 1921.

During a break in negotiations the two leaders posed for press photographs.

(1) R. C. BARTON.   (2) E. J. DUGGAN.   (3) ARTHUR GRIFFITHS.
(4) MICHAEL COLLINS.   (5) GAVAN DUFFY.

Pictured on this postcard are the five members of the Irish negotiating team that secured the terms of Irish independence.

Though the initial talks had not proved fruitful both sides needed a solution, the British more so than the Irish. The problem of Irish Independence was not going to go away, Lloyd George was having a tough time politically, and he needed a result to keep his premiership afloat.

It was agreed that an Irish delegation should again be sent to London with the power to negotiate "a Treaty between Ireland and the community of nations known as the British Commonwealth". De Valera was to take no part in the talks but remain in Dublin. To put Ireland's case he sent Arthur Griffith, Michael Collins, Robert Barton, George Gavan Duffy and Eamon Duggan. The delegation was to have the powers of plenipotentiaries. Collins was unhappy at being sent, citing that he was a soldier not a politician. The delegation proposed by de Valera was sanctioned by the Dail on 14th September. Also included in the delegation was Collins' personal secretary, Kathleen McKenna, three other secretaries, an adviser on constitutional law, John Chartres and Erskine Childers who acted as secretary to the delegation.

As with all negotiations, wording and nuances are of the upmost importance. On 29th September Lloyd George wrote to de Valera stating that he could not accept the term Irish Republic, but none the less talks began in earnest on 11th October. On the part of the British the Treaty's main objective was to end the war, on the part of the Irish it was the formation of their own state. As all is fair in love and war, Lloyd George was always keen to remind the Irish delegation that should these talks fail it would mean a return to war, which neither side wanted. An aeroplane was on permanent standby at Croydon Airport, ready to take Collins home to Ireland should the need arise. The discussions were long and tedious and every "i" had to be dotted and every "t" crossed. At the end of each day the British delegation went to their respective homes. The Irish delegation were accommodated at 22 Hans Place, Knightsbridge, just behind Harrods. There were informal meetings between the delegates of both sides and social gatherings took place especially on the part of the Irish delegation who were feted by prominent Irish living in London. George Bernard Shaw and the famous Irish portrait painter, Sir John Lavery, and his wife Hazel extended the hand of welcome and hospitality. Lady Lavery was a beautiful woman and charming hostess and it was said that during the course of the negotiations she and Collins had an affair. Hazel Lavery's portrait was seen on Irish banknotes where she is depicted as Kathleen ni Houlihan.

As plenipotentiaries the Irish delegation had the power to negotiate and conclude an agreement with the British Government, but this was the cause for much debate as they had to consult with Dublin before reaching a final decision on any big question. This seeming contradiction or ambiguity left the delegation on very shaky ground. So with the terms in position the "Articles of Agreement for a Treaty between Great Britain and Ireland", as the talks were officially known, were under way. There were several contentious points: Ireland was to become a self-governing state within the British Empire like Australia, Canada and New Zealand; the King and his successors were to be Head of State and would appoint a Governor General; members of the Irish Parliament would have to take an Oath of Allegiance to the Free State and be "faithful to His Majesty the King George V"; Northern Ireland was to have the option to withdraw from the Free State within one month of the formation of the Irish Free State; a Boundary Commission would be set up to review the borders; for the safety of Great Britain it would retain four Treaty ports.

The tedious negotiations continued during October and November often into the long, dark, dank nights of an English autumn. The Irish delegation was under great pressure not only from its own government but also from the British team who needed the talks to reach a conclusion. The biggest stumbling blocks for the Irish delegation were Oath of Allegiance, the situation of the six counties in Northern Ireland and the position of Dominion status within the Commonwealth. Lloyd George made it clear there would be no movement on the Oath. He fobbed off Griffiths with a Border Commission on the Northern Ireland position and in his own inimitable way underplayed the Dominion status. Over all this was the continued threat that if the Treaty was not signed a state of war would exist and commence within three days. Lloyd George also over-played the fact that if the signing did not take place it was most likely that his government would fail and be replaced by a Unionist anti-Irish government led by Bonar Law who had made his position on Ireland quite clear and which Griffith and Collins well knew. The two leaders of the Irish delegation were aware that the terms being offered were not the full extent of their demands but accepted that they were the best that would be offered. Their task was now to persuade the other members of the delegation to sign. So it was at 2.20 a.m. on 6th December 1921 the Treaty was signed and Rialtar Sealadac na heireann (Provisional Government of Ireland) was born, a birth that was to unleash death in the new State.

122

IRISH PEACE CONFERENCE, JULY 1921.   Delegates entering Mansion House, Dublin, on their return from London.
E. & S Ltd., Dublin]   [Photo, Hogan, Dublin.

This photograph shows de Valera and the original delegation cheered on as they enter the Mansion House in Dublin. Following on behind de Valera are: (to his left) Larry O'Neil, the Lord Mayor of Dublin; Robert Barton, in a light coloured Homburg, and directly behind him, George Gavan Duffy.

IRISH PEACE CONFERENCE, JULY, 1921.   Gathering at the Mansion House.
E. & S. Ltd.. Dublin]   Photo, Hogan. Dublin.

Dubliners mill about the main entrance of the Mansion House waiting for any news and to catch a glimpse of the delegations.

IRISH PEACE CONFERENCE, JULY, 1921.   Reciting the Rosary outside Mansion House.
E. & S. Ltd., Dublin]   [Photo, Hogan, Dublin]

Such was the devotion to Our Lady, the Mother of God and the desperation of the people that recitation of the Rosary was said, led as always by the women.

Robert Childers Barton

Robert Childers Barton came from a wealthy Protestant family and was educated in England. He was an officer in the British army stationed at Richmond Barracks, Dublin and was elected to the first Dail as Sinn Fein candidate for West Wicklow. He lost his seat in the 1923 elections and turned to the law and became a barrister and eventually a judge. He was the last of the delegation to die, on 10th August 1957.

Eamon John Duggan

Eamon John Duggan was a solicitor who fought in the Easter Rising. After his release from detention he returned to the law. He was appointed Director of Intelligence for the I.R.A. and elected to the Dail for South Meath in 1918. He was Parliamentary Secretary to the Executive Council. In 1933 he became a Senator of Seanad Eireann and he died in Dun Laoghaire on 6th June 1936.

George Gavan Duffy

George Gavan Duffy, born in Cheshire, had practised law in London and was part of Casement's defence team. He settled in Dublin in 1917 and was elected as the Sinn Fein candidate for South County Down. He was sent to the Paris Peace Talks at the end of the First World War to seek independence status for Ireland. He reluctantly accepted the Treaty and served as Minister of Foreign Affairs, resigning at the outbreak of the Civil War. He returned to his law practice and was an adviser to the Irish Government. In 1946 he was appointed President of the High Court and died at Terenure on 10th June 1951.

Passionate as the Irish delegates were, they had to negotiate with formidable and experienced British politicians. On his team Lloyd George had assembled F.E. Smith, Lord Birkenhead, Winston Churchill, Sir Harmer Greenwood, Austen Chamberlain, L. Worthington Evans and Gordon Hewart.

David Lloyd George

David Lloyd George, known as the "Welsh Wizard" because of his negotiation skills, was born in Manchester on 17th January 1863 but was brought up in Caernarvonshire. His father died when he was only one year old and his uncle became his guiding light. He was educated locally and qualified as a solicitor, setting up his own practice in the back room of his uncle's house. His practice grew and he opened offices in local towns but was now beginning to become politically active. In 1890 he won the seat of Caernarvon in a by-election, a seat he held for 55 years. He spoke out for Wales and Welsh Nationalism.

The Rt. Hon. D. Lloyd George. This is an earnest looking portrait of the young "Welsh Wizard" who by the time of the Treaty negotiations had white flowing locks. The photograph was taken at the studio of Mills and the postcard published by Raphael Tuck & Sons.

He continued to practise as a solicitor and opened a firm in London whilst his reputation in the Liberal Party ranks grew, gaining notoriety for his outspoken attack on the 2nd Boer War. When he verbally attacked Joseph Chamberlain in a speech in Birmingham he had to be smuggled out of the meeting disguised as a policeman. In 1906 he became President of the Board of Trade and two years later Chancellor of the Exchequer, a position he held until 1915 during which time he introduced the State Pension (old age pension) and National Insurance. His 1911 radical budget was just as controversial, introducing tax on unearned income and raising inheritance tax. In 1915 he was made Minister for Munitions and in 1916 Secretary of State for War. On 7th December 1916 he became an effective, though at times autocratic, Prime Minister. His negotiation skills came to the fore when dealing with the Irish Delegation during the Treaty Talks.

He remained leader of the Liberal Party until 1931 and was Father of the House from 1929-1945. Lloyd was a recognised womaniser despite remaining married to his wife Margaret until her death in 1941. To the consternation of his children two years later he married his secretary and mistress, Frances Stevenson, with whom it is said he had been in a relationship since 1913. Lloyd George was feted with many honours and academic degrees, the last of which came on 1st January 1945 when he was enobled Earl Lloyd George of Dwyfor. He died three months later on 26th March 1945.

Winston Leonard Spencer Churchill

Winston Leonard Spencer Churchill was born prematurely at Blenheim Palace, Woodstock in Oxfordshire on 30th November 1874. From the age of two until six years old he grew up in Dublin where his father was secretary to his grandfather who was Viceroy of Ireland. He attended three primary schools before finally going to Harrow. He managed, at a third attempt, to get into Sandhurst where he finally got a commission as a second lieutenant in the 4th Queens Own Horse. He resigned from the army in 1899 and stood for election at Oldham where he failed to get elected but he gained the post of war correspondent at the *Morning Post* to cover the 2nd Boer War. He was taken prisoner, but escaped and rejoined the army and was one of the first to re-enter Ladysmith. In the 1900 election he

A young Winston Churchill.

again stood as a Conservative candidate for Oldham and this time was succesful. In 1904 he crossed the floor to the Liberal Party and was appointed Under Secretary of State for the Colonies, only to return to the Conservatives at a later date. During this period Churchill held almost every post in the cabinet: Home Secretary, First Lord of the Admiralty, Minister for Munitions, Secretary of State for War, Secretary of State for the Air, Chancellor of the Exchequer and finally, at Britain's most vulnerable time, Prime Minster during the Second World War. Regarding Ireland he was prepared to blockade the northern ports during the Home Rule Crisis and he advocated using all force during the Irish War of Independence. He sat on the Treaty team and it is said he struck up a relationship with Collins, but it did not stop him from later threatening to use British forces to bring the Civil War to a conclusion if Collins did not sort out the situation.

Churchill's life was lived to the full and he was never afraid to speak his mind, sometimes to his detriment. He was also a prolific author, writing many definitive works and was awarded the Nobel Prize for Literature in 1953. He was also the first person made an Honorary Citizen of the United States of America. In 1922 he bought his family home in Chartwell, Kent where in later life he took up oil painting. Dying on 24th January 1965 in London he was honoured with a State Funeral and is buried in St. Martins Church, Blandon, Oxfordshire.

Fredrick Edward Smith

Lord Birkenhead was born Fredrick Edward Smith in Birkenhead, Cheshire in 1872. He was educated locally and finished his education studying law at Wadham College, Oxford. He soon acquired a reputation as a formidable

9402 A   MR. F. E. SMITH, K.C., M.P.   ROTARY PHOTO, E.C.

This portrait shows a young Mr. Smith, who was later made Lord Birkenhead. The photograph of Smith was taken by Reginald Haines and the postcard published by Rotary.

advocate with a quick wit and ascerbic tongue. He moved to London where he became one of the highest paid barristers, covering many high profile cases including the successful defence for murder of Ethel Le Nerve, Crippen's mistress. In 1916 he was the lead prosecutor at the trial of Sir Roger Casement.

He entered Parliament representing Walton in 1906 and by 1915 was Attorney General. In 1919 he was made Lord Chancellor. Vehemently opposed to Home Rule he supported Carson and the movement against it.

He drafted most of the 1921 Anglo Irish Treaty and to the disgust of his Ulster friends built up a relationship with Michael Collins to the extent that at the end of the negotiations he is reported to have said to Collins "I may just have signed my political death warrant". Having served in the Lloyd George coalitions in 1924 he was made Secretary of State for India. By now his dependence on alcohol was a problem, causing cirrhosis of the liver, pneumonia and finally his death at the age of 58 in London in 1930. It was said of him that "F. E. Smith is very clever, but sometimes his brains go to his head".

Hamar Greenwood

Hamar Greenwood was a Canadian lawyer who was born on 7th February 1870 in Whitby, Ontario, Canada. He was elected as a Liberal M.P. for York in 1906 and in 1910 for Sunderland until 1922. From 1924 he was M.P. for Walthamstow East for five years. During this time he held the post of Under Secretary of State for the Home Department and then Secretary for Overseas Trade. As Chief Secretary for Ireland from 1920–1922, the last person to hold the post, he was included in the Treaty talks. At this time he was part of the Cabinet and a Privy Counsellor. An advocate of the use of force by the Black and Tans and the Auxiliaries during the War of Independence, he claimed the burning of Cork by British troops was the work of the I.R.A. He was created Baron Greenwood in 1929 and held several high profile posts after leaving politics. He died on 10th September 1948.

Gordon Hewart

Gordon Hewart was born in Bury, Lancashire on 7th January 1870 and was educated at Bury Grammar School and University College, Oxford. From 1913 he was the Liberal M.P. for Leicester and in 1918 was made a Privy Counsellor. The following year he was made Attorney General and it was in this role that he took part in the Treaty negotiations. In 1921 he was a member of the Cabinet. He was made Lord Chief Justice of England and Wales in 1922 (a post he held until 1940) as well as being made Baron Hewart. A believer of true justice, in 1931 with two other judges, he quashed a murder conviction because of lack of evidence. He was the originator of the phrase "Not only must Justice be done; it must also be seen to be done". Hewart died in Totteridge, Hertfordshire (now part of North London) on 5th May 1943.

Sir L. (Laming) Worthington-Evans

Sir L. (Laming) Worthington-Evans was born on 23rd August 1868 and became a solicitor. In 1910 he won the seat of Colchester for the Conservatives which he held until 1929 when he won the seat of Westminster St. George's. He held a commission in the 2nd Middlesex Artillery Volunteers during the First World War and served as a temporary major. He was made Baronet of Colchester in 1916. In Lloyd George's coalition government he held the position of Secretary of State at the Ministry of Munitions and Minister of Blockade. At the end of the war he became Minister of Pensions and sat on the Treaty team as Secretary of State for War, an office he returned to in 1924 and held until 1929. In between he was Postmaster-General for a year in 1923-24 and was editor of the *Financial News* during 1924-25. He died at the age of 62 on 14th February 1931.

Austen Chamberlain

Austen Chamberlain was born on 16th October 1863 in Birmingham, the son of Joseph the leading figure in Liberal politics at the turn of the century. He was educated at Rugby School and Trinity College Cambridge after which he spent two years in Paris and Germany. Returning to England in 1892 he won the seat of East Worcestershire thanks to his father's influence. His maiden speech was acclaimed by no less that William Ewart Gladstone as "one of the best speeches which has been made". In 1895 he was appointed Civil Lord of the Admiralty, a post he held for five years. During the following 31 years he held almost every high office with the exception of Prime Minster. He was Chancellor of the Exchequer twice, Secretary of State for India, Postmaster General, Foreign Secretary, Lord Privy Seal, First Lord of the Admiralty and Leader of the Conservative Party. He was also vehemently opposed to the Third Home Rule Bill and was part of the British team at the Treaty talks. In 1929 he became a back bencher who together with Churchill warned of the serious threat of German rearmament. He died on 17th March 1937 at the age of 73, just ten weeks before his half-brother Neville Chamberlain became Prime Minister.

SCOTT SERIES
Nº 929 B   MR AUSTEN CHAMBERLAIN.   SCOTT RUSSELL & CO
                                                        BIRMINGHAM

This is a portrait of a young Austen Chamberlain who was one of a famous political dynasty which included his father Joseph and step brother Neville.

Chapter 12: Civil War

The Irish delegation returned to Dublin amidst great jubilation but with doubts that their deliberations would be universally accepted. The Treaty document was presented to the cabinet on 8th December where it was only passed by four votes: Griffith, Collins, Barton and Cosgrove to the three against de Valera, Brugha and Stack. De Valera in particular was vehemently opposed to the terms and published a paper repudiating it. None the less the document was put forward for debate in the Dail, which turned out to be long, bitter and personal. Members often attacked each other more so than the Treaty, a sign of things to come. The debate lasted through the Christmas period and early into the new year until on 7th January 1922 the Dail carried the motion of accepting the Treaty by 64 votes to 57.

The general public, weary of the fighting, welcomed the news and the recognition of the Provisional Government. De Valera was not so enthusiastic and refused to accept the vote in favour of the Treaty and the Provisional Government. He resigned as President and led his followers from the Dail. Griffith was elected President and Collins became Chairman of the Government.

With the Provisional Government in administrative control the long slog to set up the offices of state began. In a room in the Shelbourne Hotel members of the government met to draw up a constitution in what today is called the Constitution Room. Piece by piece the transfer of powers were handed over to the new Provisional Government.

The last Lord Lieutenant of Ireland, Viscount Fitzalan of Derwent left Dublin Castle as did British troops for the last time after 700 years. On 16th June a general election was held when over 620,000 votes were cast. The Treaty candidates polled over 239,000 votes, the anti-Treaty candidates received over 140,000 votes and close on 250,000 votes were cast for other candidates. The Dail was now made up of 58 pro-Treaty T.D.s, 35 anti-Treaty, seventeen Labour seats, while the other eighteen seats were taken up by the other three smaller parties.

As civil wars go the Irish Civil War was short but like most civil wars it was violent and left deep scars that took generations to heal. It was an I.R.A. war, the I.R.A. forces against the Treaty versus the I.R.A. forces for the Treaty, now called the National Army.

The anti-Treaty forces had Liam Lynch as their military leader and Joseph McKelvey as the deputy Chief of Staff and de Valera their political leader. The Treaty forces were the National Army of the Government that was led by the Minister of Defence, Richard Mulcahy and Eoin O'Duffy, their Chief of Staff. Their political leader was Liam Cosgrave. The sides were now drawn up for the impending Civil War that in fairness to the government was delayed until the last minute.

The Civil War was triggered by the seizure of the Four Courts on 13th April 1922 by an anti-Treaty force led by Oscar Traynor. The government were loathe to act against them but pressurised by Churchill, who was prepared to send in British troops to settle the situation. O'Duffy began an offensive against them on 28th June, using field guns supplied to them by the British Army.

> *England gave the orders, and gave the cannon too*
> *And Michael sent the boys in green to conquer Cathal Brugha*
> *For England's bloody must be satisfied anew*
> *For England gave the orders, and gave the cannon too.*

(a popular ditty of the time)

From across the River Liffey the artillery fired with impunity and in relative safety whilst all the anti-Treaty forces could offer in reply were rifle bullets. Within two days the garrison was forced to surrender, though not before they had destroyed many of the historical records held in the building. The most devastating part of the action for the anti-Treaty forces was the capture of many of their most important leaders – Rory O'Connor, Liam Mellows, Dick Barrett, Ernie O'Malley and Joseph McKelvey.

This card shows smoke rising from the fire that engulfed the Four Courts.

E. & S., Ltd., D.]   Military Operations, Dublin, June~July, 1922.   [Photo, Hogan, Dublin.
NATIONAL FORCES FIRING FROM ROYAL BANK OF IRELAND, O'CONNELL ST.

The National Army had to fight house by house to clear the I.R.A. from some parts of Dublin.

E. & S., Ltd. (D.]   Military Operations, Dublin, June~July 1922.   [Photo, Hogan, Dublin.
NATIONAL ARMY RESERVES AT BARRICADE.

A flimsy barricade is all that protects the 'Treaty' forces against a possible attack whilst all around is scattered paper.

Though the Four Courts had been taken this was not the end of the fighting in Dublin. The anti-Treaty forces still remained a threat in the city and soon occupied the Hamman Hotel and other buildings in the area which became collectively known as "the block". Here the anti-Treaty forces battled it out with the National Army, with no real hope of winning. Eventually Brugha ordered his garrison to evacuate the buildings and on the 7th July he exited the building, firing at the government forces in a final last act of rebellion and was shot dead.

E. & S., Ltd., D.] Military Operations, Dublin, June-July, 1922. [Photo, Hogan, D.
NATIONAL FORCES BOMBING HAMMAM HOTEL.

Upper O'Connell Street, Dublin, after the fighting 1922.

By and large the city had been cleared of anti-Treaty forces and battle-worn and scarred Dublin could for the second time start to rebuild itself.

For the next months anti-Treaty forces took control of several towns and cities including Limerick. Here Lynch had set up his headquarters and with the support of other anti-Treaty units in the area was in a strong position, controlling the major barracks in the city. He also had a tacit agreement with Michael Brennan, the local Treaty commander, not to attack each other thereby avoiding a civil war. Limerick was crucial to both sides and it would not be overstating the fact that whoever held the city would ultimately win the war. Lynch believed that by holding a truce he would avoid a war, which offended his strong religious principles but militarily would tie up the National Army, whilst enabling him to move his forces from the city to strengthen more vulnerable positions. The truce between the two commanders was a "pie in the sky" idea which although honest in its intention was never going to happen. Whether the truce entered into by Brennan was a ploy by him to buy time for the ill-equipped National Army is unsure, but on 11th July Dublin despatched 150 well-armed men to the city and Brennan officially informed Lynch that the treaty had been terminated over the shooting of a National Army soldier. Further military supplies soon arrived so that now the National Army had a greater advantage in military hardware over the anti-Treaty forces.

On 4th July the Millmount Fort at Drogheda was captured by the National Army under the command of Ned Stapleton.

On 19th July 18lb guns fired on the Strand Barracks from across the Shannon. A fight was pointless and slowly the anti-Treaty forces retreated, but not before setting fire to the barracks. By the following day Limerick was in the hands of the National Army.

NATIONAL TROOPS SEARCHING CIVILIANS.

Cork, like Limerick, was another anti-Treaty stronghold. The city was under the control of the anti-Treaty forces who in a propaganda effort took over the *Cork Examiner* newspaper to get their message to the people. An uniquely conceived plan was made to take control of the city. On Bank Holiday Monday, 9th August, Emmet Dalton with 450 well-equipped National Army soldiers landed at Passage West. Expecting an attack, the anti-Treaty forces had prepared themselves for an overland offensive, but they were not prepared for an attack from the sea. Nonetheless they put up stiff resistance and it was three days before the city was under the control of the National Army. They found a destoyed city in the wake of the retreating foe. There was no doubt that the element of surprise played a large part in the taking of the city but it was also a well-equipped army that helped win the day.

Gradually other towns and cities throughout the country fell to the National Army, many without too much opposition. Waterford, Tralee, Tipperary, Wexford, Clonmel, Dundalk, and Kilmallock, which had a reputation over the generations for being a rebellious stronghold succumbed where an organised resistance might have won the day. At these locations the anti-Treaty forces disappeared without so much as a fight and the towns were reoccupied by the National Army and came under the control of the Government.

Unable to take on the Treaty forces in a full battle the anti-Treaty forces did as they had done during the War of Independence and took to the hills. From here they fought a guerrilla war of ambush and reprisal and destruction, seemingly without any real aim except to inflict embarrassment on the National Army.

The anti-Treaty forces were battle hardened men but even they were now tiring of living out in the field without any cover, having to scavenge for food from a population that was also tired of the fighting and barely able to scratch a living from the land themselves without some starving force swooping down to steal a chicken or eggs. In the majority of cases the anti-Treaty forces did not have the backing of the population they had enjoyed during the War of Independence.

Whilst there were no major conflicts, the sniping and skirmishing still took place with the anti-Treaty forces disrupting the lives of citizens. The blowing up of bridges, railway or other types across rivers seemed their logic to try to win the war. In truth they had no plan and often no strategy in their efforts to defeat the National Army. There was little or no communication between the divisional commandants. With the war seemingly petering out reprisals and settling of old scores were now becoming commonplace. In response to the murder of Sean Hales, T.D., and a Treaty supporter, the Government executed Rory O'Connor, Richard Barrett, Liam Mellows and Joseph McKelvey on 8th December 1922.

On 1st February Liam Lynch sent out an order that any government T.D. was a legitimate target. During the period from November 1922 until May 1923 the Government authorised the execution of 77 anti-Treaty prisoners. An amnesty was announced by the Government and soon afterwards a group led by the bishops tried to broker a truce but without success. At a meeting held on 24th March anti-Treaty commandants met to argue the motion for a truce, which was defeated. Another meeting was arranged for 10th April but Lynch was caught and shot in the Knockmealdown mountain by soldiers of the National Army. He was taken to Clonmel Hospital where that evening he died of his wounds. In the following weeks more of the anti-Treaty commandants were taken prisoner which led to the announcement of a ceasefire that was to take effect from noon on the 30th April. In the days that followed the "dumping of arms" other contentious matters were discussed until on 24th May de Valera conceded defeat.

The bitter war was over. Anti-Treaty forces quietly slipped back to their homes bowed but not defeated, prepared to take up arms again for the republic that eventually came.

Official figures state that 11,316 Republican prisoners were arrested, most of whom were released within the year. Approximately six to seven hundred died during the struggle. The financial cost to the country as a whole was estimated at 50 million pounds. But this was nothing as to the deep division that the war caused to the population as a whole, a division that still holds today in certain quarters. Time is a great healer and after waiting so long for its independence Ireland has plenty of time for the healing yet to do.

Liam Lynch

Lynch was born near Mitchelstown, Co. Cork on 9th November 1893. At the age of seventeen he joined the Gaelic League and seven years later the Fermoy I.V. In 1919 after reorganising the Cork I.V. he became commandant of 2nd Cork Brigade. During the War of Independence he gained a reputation by taking the British Army barracks at Mallow with Ernie O'Malley. With the re-organisation of the I.R.A. he was appointed Commander of the 1st Southern Division in 1921. He was opposed to the Treaty and in March 1922 became Chief of Staff of the anti-Treaty forces. He was arrested in June 1922 in Dublin but released on the proviso that he use his influence to stop the fighting.

Now in opposition to the government he planned to set up a Munster Republic to hinder the government. This would be defended by the "Limerick Waterford Line" along the major towns and cities he hoped to control. With the fall of Limerick he moved his headquarters to Fermoy.

When Cork was taken by the National Army he had to abandon Fermoy and adopt guerrilla tactics. In reprisal to government executions he issued orders that government supporters and various dignitaries were now "fair game" and a series of killings and attacks on property were sanctioned. He was criticised for his lack of co-ordination of the war by the anti-Treaty forces which led to the guerrilla tactics. The struggle wore on and victory appeared less likely and on 10th April he was shot and died in hospital at Clonmel. He is buried in Kilcrumper Cemetery near Fermoy, Co. Cork.

Joseph McKelvey

Joseph McKelvey was known to most as Joe. He was born in Stewartstown, Co. Tyrone. He was an Irish language student and trained as an accountant before working for the Income Tax Office in Belfast where he joined the I.V. and the I.R.B. He took part in the War of Independence where he commanded the unit that burnt the Income Tax Office.

His Catholic faith and his Nationalist beliefs like so many others in Belfast were the cause of his dismissal from his employment. In August 1920 he organised the killing of an R.I.C. detective which caused the burning of Catholic homes in Lisburn. By March 1921 he was appointed commander of 3rd Northern Division of the I.R.A., his job made the more difficult for fear that any attack against the state would result in reprisal against Catholics. He opposed the Treaty, left the 3rd Division and joined the anti-Treaty I.R.A. He was taken prisoner when the Four Courts fell and was held for five months in Mountjoy Prison until his execution on 8th December 1922 together with Barrett, Mellows and O'Connor.

Rory O'Connor

Rory O'Connor was born in Dublin on 8th December 1883 and educated at University College gaining a degree in arts and engineering. He spent four years in Canada working as a railway engineer. Returning to Ireland in 1915 he joined the I.R.B. and during the Easter Rising was wounded. During the War of Independence he worked as Director of Engineering but when it came he opposed the Treaty and became chairman of the Military Council of the anti-Treaty I.R.A. He was a leading member of the Four Courts Garrison where he was captured when it fell to the National Army and heralded the outbreak of the Civil War. He was held in Mountjoy Prison until his execution on 8th December. O'Connor's execution order was signed by the Minister of Justice, Kevin O'Higgins, who less than a year before had O'Connor as his best man at his wedding.

Richard Barrett

Richard Barrett was born on 17th December 1889 in Knockacullen, Co. Cork. He trained as a teacher and in 1914 was appointed principal of Gurrane National School. He joined the G.A.A. and by 1917 was a member of the I.V. and Sinn Fein. Later he joined the I.R.B. and organised fund-raising events in order to buy weapons. In April of 1921 he was arrested and sent to Spike Island, where he was one of the senior officers. With six other officers he escaped in November of that year. He strongly opposed the Treaty and joined O'Connor in taking the Four Courts. When the Four Courts were taken he like all the other prisoners was held in Mountjoy Prison and like the other leaders was executed on 8th December 1922 at 2 a.m. on the orders of the Minister of Justice, Kevin O'Higgins.

Chapter 13: Ten Days in August

Within ten days in August 1922 the fledgling Provisional Government suffered the dual blow of the death of two of its most prominent politicians.

ARTHUR GRIFFITH, T.D.,
Elected President, Dail Eireann, January, 1922.
Died 12th August, 1922.

A not unfamiliar portrait of Griffith wearing as ever his Deanta in Eirinn tie identified by the white emblem in the knot.

Arthur Griffith, the newspaper proprietor, who through his publications urged and argued his countrymen to proclaim their birthright to a free and independent state was the first of these influential men to die. The avuncular figure with his Deanta in Eirinn (made in Ireland) tie, who so influenced the formation of Sinn Fein, who led the Irish delegation in the Peace Talks at the end of the Irish War of Independence and then took on the role of President when de Valera walked out of the Dail on 7th January. The heavy workload of the negotiations plus the bitter debate in the Dail, coupled with the responsibility of setting up the Government of a new country, took its toll on his health. Early in August 1922 he entered St. Vincent's Nursing Home, where doctors diagnosed his illness as subarachnoid haemorrhage and confined him to a private room for total rest. Mindful of his position and the responsibilities that the office held this conscientious man returned to his work sooner than he ought.

At the Government Buildings on 12th August at about 10 o'clock he fell and became unconscious. He regained conciousness but leaving the building he collapsed again. Doctors and a priest were called but this time he could not be revived.

He was the first Irish President to be buried as the Head of State. After a funeral Mass at the Pro-Cathedral on 16th August his cortege was taken to Glasnevin where his body was interred. Though he did not fight for his country with a gun, as many before him had done, he fought and paid the price with his life at the age of 50 for the country he loved.

The postcard shows the imposing building designed by Sir Aston Webb that was opened in 1911. In 1922 it was the home of most government ministers and their families as a safeguard against anti-Treaty reprisals.

THE FUNERAL OF THE LATE PRESIDENT ARTHUR GRIFFITH.   LEAVING THE CATHEDRAL.

Griffith's coffin draped in the tricolour is carried down the steps of the Pro-Cathedral to the awaiting gun carriage destined for Glasnevin. This is a Hely's postcard.

FUNERAL OF THE LATE PRESIDENT ARTHUR GRIFFITH.   PASSING THROUGH O'CONNELL STREET.

Plumed horses pull a carriage of principal mourners while the street is thronged with Dubliners respectful of the event.

The Pro-Cathedral is sited at the corner of Marlborough Street and Cathedral Street (formerly Elephant Lane) where mass has been held since 1825.

THE FUNERAL OF THE LATE PRESIDENT ARTHUR GRIFFITH.   AT THE GRAVESIDE.

A firing party from the National Army fires a salvo while altar boys cover their ears. Michael Collins stands at the left of this view and behind him is Daryl Figgis and Liam Cosgrove.

FUNERAL OF THE LATE PRESIDENT ARTHUR GRIFFITH.   HIS GRACE THE ARCHBISHOP OF DUBLIN AFTER THE FINAL BLESSING.

The clergy gather around the coffin of Arthur Griffith as the Archbishop of Dublin, Edward Byrne administers the final blessing, 16th August 1922.

Collins was now de facto Prime Minister of the country, right in the centre of things, pulling all the strings, just as he had done in Frongoch and during the War of Independence.

GENERAL MICHAEL COLLINS, T.D.,
Commander-in-Chief National Army,
Killed in Ambush, Co. Cork, 22nd August, 1922.

E. & S. Ltd. D.   Photo. HOGAN, DUBLIN

This postcard shows Collins in his uniform of Commander-in-Chief of the National Army.

An intelligent man whose stature demanded respect, Collins had been Joseph Plunkett's aide during the Easter Rising. It was in North Wales in the Frongoch concentration camp that his charisma and organisational skills came to the fore. At the "University of Revolution" at Frongoch he built up his network of contacts and a reputation that was to serve him and his country well during the struggle against the British in the War of Independence.

Collins was part of the Irish delegation to the Peace Conference. Ever the realist, he and the delegation returned to Dublin with an imperfect Treaty, the best that was available but one which would eventually lead to independence. The bitter Dail debate over and won, he set about the formation of the Government where he played a pivotal role.

The Civil War seemingly over, or at least coming to a close, he took it upon himself to visit his home county of Cork, which many still considered "bandit" country. Despite voiced misgivings he went ahead with the visit. No one was going to harm him in his native county was the gist of his response to these misgivings. How wrong he was!

On 22nd August 1922 at 6.30 a.m. a small convoy with a scout motorbike at its head, followed by a Crossley tender with riflemen, an open tourer carrying Collins and Emett Dalton, the local National Army commander and a Rolls

Royce armoured car left the Imperial Hotel, Cork and headed towards Macroom. Heading along the Bandon road they passed through Beal na Blath. Uncertain of the route the convoy stopped to ask for directions. Unknown to them an anti-Treaty I.R.A. man who recognised the occupants of the tourer notified his colleagues of the convoy and its occupants. In the hope that the convoy would return by the same route an ambush was set up at Beal na Blath. At about 8 o'clock that evening the convoy indeed returned the way it came and ran into the ambush. Rather than drive through as fast as they could Collins ordered the convoy to stop and return fire.

According to reports, Collins was standing returning fire without cover when he was hit. Dragged to the tourer and cradled in Emett Dalton's arms the order was now given to head for Cork at speed. With night fast drawing in the convoy again got lost and did not arrive in Cork until 1.30 a.m. on 23rd August where Collins was officially pronounced dead at Shanakkiel Hospital. His body was loaded onto a ship and taken around the coast to Dublin for fear that his cortege would be attacked if it were taken over land. In Dublin his body lay in state for three days in City Hall and then like Griffith's it was taken to the Pro-Cathedral on 28th August for a requiem mass that was attended by dignitaries from home and abroad.

FUNERAL OF THE LATE GENERAL MICHAEL COLLINS.   IN THE PRO-CATHEDRAL.

This postcard shows the interior of the Pro-Cathedral with Collins' coffin draped in the tricolour at the altar rails.

The passing of these two men placed a great responsibility on the new leaders, in particular Cosgrave and Mulcahy who had to lead the Provisional Government through some very dark times.

As with many who die young (Collins was only 32 years old when he was killed) legends and myths grow about them. How many are true hardly seems to matter, we seem to enjoy them all the more if they are tinged with doubt. What does appear to be true is that in Collins' case at least, he is a bigger legend now than during his brief life.

"It is my considered opinion that in the fullness of time, history will record the greatness of Collins and it will be recorded at my expense" – Eamon de Valera.

Chapter 14: Publishers

The Easter Rising fell into a period known as the "Golden Age of the Postcard" when any topic no matter how small was captured by some publisher and produced in postcard form. Postcards were popular because they were easy and cheap to produce, available everywhere, cost little to buy and post and in an age when postal services were what they said they were, a service assured of delivery. Postcards were not only used as a means of communication but also bought as items worthy of collection.

The publishers of the postcards that depict the Easter Rising are like life in general, many and various, large and small. They range from international postcard publishers like Valentine's and Rotary to small local publishers like Keohan. Many famous names produced these postcards but few have survived to now. Valentine's were bought up by Hallmark in the 1970s, Woolworth went into administration and many others ceased trading for one reason or another. What is common to them all is the history, the evidence of the birth of a new country, Ireland. Today we have devices that record for us any event that can be captured by a camera and the footage is the cine film for the newsreels of the future. But footage has one failing, it is not tactile. When you hold an original postcard from any era you are holding the history of that era, but when the publishers produced these postcards they probably did not think like that. They just saw an opportunity to make money and the Easter Rising gave them the chance to do so. The following companies produced postcards during this era and on this subject and will be listed in alphabetical order.

Albert

A Belgian company. I have two postcards, one of de Valera and one of John Redmond. I find it rather odd that a Belgian company should produce postcards of Irishmen.

Left: **This postcard shows a grim looking de Valera. I am at a loss why a Belgium company would issue a card of an Irish politician. The back states "Phototypie A. Dohmen Bruxelles".**

Right: **John Redmond. A relaxed looking Redmond in later life.**

W & G Baird

In 1861 two brothers, William Savage Baird and George Courtney Baird, bought the liquidated Ulster Printing Co. of Arthur Street, Belfast for £450. William, 38 had been employed by the company and George, 29 was an overseer at the *Daily Mercury*. The new company began trading in 1862 and soon built up a reputation as jobbing printers. On 1st September 1862 they printed the first edition of *The Belfast Telegraph* and four years later in 1866 published their own broadsheet *The Belfast Election*. After a long illness George Baird died on 14th April 1875. His place in the firm was taken by his brother, Thomas Drew Baird. In 1870 Baird installed the first rotary press in Belfast. In 1886 the business moved to new premises at the junction of Royal Avenue and Little Donegal Street, but 23 days after the move William Savage Baird died, on 21st July 1886. On 5th April 1890 W&G Baird became a limited company.

By 1894 the first typesetting machine was installed and process engraving was installed in 1898. By 1903 Baird were considered Ulster's leading printers and had offices in Dublin and London. The business continued to grow, always under the control of the family, several of whom were knighted. After a period of internal problems the company was bought by Lord Thompson in September 1961. Ten years later the factory was blown up by the I.R.A. and a new one was built in Antrim in 1977. That same year there was a management buy-out and the business expanded into packaging as well as retaining their place as Belfast's premier printers.

It is generally accepted that Baird published only six views of the Rising, all of which are of the ruins and all of which show Dubliners discussing the dramatic events that turned their city to rubble. All the Baird views have a white band at the base of the card which carries the caption and the name W&G Baird Ltd Belfast. Only one carries the name Baird in the view. Whether all the views are copyright to Baird and this one is not, or when printed it was forgotten to print the name is open for conjecture. Three of the views are attributable to T.W. Murphy as they appear in his book *Dublin After the Six Days Insurrection* that was published by Mercredy, Percy. According to this book Mr. Murphy was the sub-editor of *The Motor News*. Like with many other publishers you could buy the six views as a pack in a special envelope. Baird also produced postcards of another form of upheaval, that of Home Rule, one of which is illustrated below.

COPYRIGHT.   DONEGALL PLACE, BELFAST, UNDER HOME RULE.

Donegal Place, Belfast, under Home Rule. This is just one of the many postcards that were published in an effort to sway public opinion against Home Rule.

City Printing Co. Limerick

City Printing Co. were long established printers who in 1913 could be found at 11 Rutland Street, Limerick. They printed a variety of cards depicting Nationalist personalities including John Daly, Captain Liam Mellows and Joseph O'Donoghue. As demands changed they produced items of a more social nature such as programmes, menus etc. well into the 1930s.

Sir Roger Casement. This photograph of Casement was taken in New York in 1914. In the original view Casement is pictured with John Devoy by his side in an open-topped carriage.

Coleman

Until a few years ago if you had walked down Westmoreland Street Dublin and stopped at No. 9 you would have been at one of the last locations where Rising postcards were printed in 1916. Today the site is occupied by a Londis store. In 1884 Coleman, or to give them their full title Thomas J. Coleman, were listed in the Dublin street directory as stationers and engravers. They also had a branch at 7 College Street, Dublin.

In 1884 engraving was carried out in the basement of No. 9 where the work was also printed. This side of the business was closed in 1967. The shop in Westmoreland Street was sold by the Coleman family to a Mr. Gladdery who in turn sold the business to a partnership of Mr. Jack Morton and Mr. Arthur Gray. During all this time a link was retained with the Coleman family via a sub post office at the back of the shop that was run by Mrs. Coleman, but with her death this closed. The business was now owned by the O'Reilly family who purchased No. 8 and expanded the business selling to Dubliners and tourist alike. From all of this the conclusion is that the Coleman Rising postcards were more than likely printed in the basement of these premises. For such a small company Coleman published a wide range of Rising postcards. Their views fall into three categories of 'Destruction', 'Ephemera' and 'Personalities'.

Sackville Street and O'Connell Bridge, Dublin, Before the Rising, 1916.

This is an example of how publishers could turn an ordinary view card into a Rising postcard by adding the last three words. Many publishers did this.

'Destruction' covers all the main sites of the Rising plus a view card of Sackville Street with added wording, 'Before the Rising 1916'. I am only aware of eleven views in this series but cards were mostly issued in dozens or groups of six. These same views were printed in two other formats. In the first format the views were printed in monochrome and had the added wording "after the bombardment". Some of these views were also printed in light shades of sepia. The third form of these views was printed in a strong sepia and the typeface of the caption was more bold; here the captions clearly stated "after the Bombardment". The Ephemera section contain views of documents which are some of the most interesting cards produced of the Rising; eight cards fall into this category. The views depicted on these cards contain what are probably the two most important documents of Irish history, the Proclamation and the Surrender documents. These also come in both monochrome and sepia. The third category of Personalities show the expected portraits of the Rising's leaders; these are all in a sepia tone.

The cards mentioned above all bear the name Coleman on the back, but Coleman produced two other forms of their postcards. Using the original views they produced a set of cards in a Terra Cotta coloured ink with a 'back' (the address side) printed in green but with no publishers name on it. The other set is of unnamed postcards which again uses the original set of views in their monochrome form with identical captions. The backing, again printed in green, gives no indication to the printer or publisher. There may be a very good reason for not printing their name on the cards. If they wished to sell their cards on to other retailers without a name it would appear the cards were from an independent publisher rather than the shop in Westmoreland Street.

J. Corringham

Like so many other retailers J. Corringham had no facilities to print postcards so they leased a couple of Valentine's views, one of which was a "BEFORE AND AFTER" card and published under their own name. Corringham were right in the centre of Dublin at 33 Eden Quay.

This sepia postcard bears the imprint Corringham on the back but is in fact a Valentine's postcard leased to them.

Craddock

Martin Craddock was a newsagent and stationer, though the backing clearly states "publisher", who traded from 17 Harcourt Road in 1916. In 1930 Craddock moved to No. 24 where they remained until 1969. In 1916 Craddock used a Valentine's view that was unlike most others that Valentine's had sold on to small retailers.

Curran

P.J. Curran had their headquarters at 4 Crow Street Dublin and after Powell Press were the largest publishers of portraits of the Easter Rising leaders. They, like all the other publishers of such cards, relied heavily on the output from the photographic studios of Keogh Brothers and Lafayette. They issued postcards on some of the lesser-known personalities like the Lawlesses and Monteith. A novelty was their Signature Series where in the caption or on the photograph of the personality was printed their signature. There was another group of postcards issued under their name but these were Valentine's views leased to them.

EAMONN CEANNT

SEAN CONNOLLY

Left: **This photograph shows Ceannt with his set of Uileann pipes. He was a skilled player and it is said that he once played for the Pope. This is an Arnall of Dublin portrait.**

Right: **Sean Connolly, aspiring actor, was the first man recorded to die for his country in the Easter Rising.**

Daily Sketch

The Daily Sketch was a British daily newspaper that was colloquially known as "the Sketch". It ceased publication on 11th May 1971. Postcards of conflicts published by newspapers were not unknown – the *Daily Mail* published postcards of scenes from the First World War. In the week preceding the Rising the Sketch, along with other newspapers, was full of the exploits of the ANZACS (Australian and New Zealand Army Corps). This all changed when on Tuesday 25th April came the reports of the arrest of Sir Roger Casement. The following day came the first reports of the Easter Rising in Dublin.

The Sketch issued two sets of postcards under their name. Both sets use the same views but vary slightly in the scope of the view and the position and style of the caption. The easiest differentiation is on the back of the cards. One set is numbered and the other is not. As an example DAILY SKETCH Copyright Photo No. 2 whilst the same view in the unnumbered set merely states "DAILY SKETCH" Copyright Photograph. In the numbered series there are sixteen views whilst in the unnumbered series there are only thirteen views. All the views are of destruction. During the Irish Civil War the Sketch used a company by the name of Maunder Brothers to supply them with photographs, so it is possible that the same firm supplied them with images for their Rising postcards. Another odd point is that in all their captions they state "May" as the time of the Rising when it began on 25th April and came to an end when Pearse signed the surrender on 29th April. The Sketch postcards are not alone in printing the wrong date in their captions.

Irish Rebellion, May, 1916.
Holding a Dublin street against the Rebels.

This is *Daily Sketch* postcard No. 2. This domestic barricade was erected at the junction of Parnell Street and Moore Street and is situated outside Simpson & Wallace, butchers at No. 57 Parnell Street. It is very probable that the block that the soldier is laying on to the right of the view came from the butchers.

Irish Rebellion_May 1916.
Holding a Dublin street against the Rebels.

This is the *Daily Sketch* unnumbered view that is equivalent to the view above and is included to show the difference between the two issues, the most obvious being the typeface used for the caption.

Irish Rebellion, May, 1916.
Liberty Hall, Dublin, the Rebel Headquarters, after the storming.

Dubliners gather in Beresford Place to see the damage. Liberty Hall was originally built as a Turkish baths. This was the view used for numbered issues.

Irish Rebellion – May 1916.
Liberty Hall, Dublin, the Rebel Headquarters, after the storming.

This is the view of Liberty Hall that was used for the *Daily Sketch* unnumbered issues, which is a totally different view from the numbered issue. The caption is misleading as Liberty Hall was never stormed. It was shelled by the gunboat *Helga* as the British believed that the Hall was heavily manned and would not risk a frontal attack.

P. J. Dooley

CAPT. THOMAS JOSEPH WAFER,
Irish Republican Army.
Killed in Action, April 26th, 1916.

Thomas Joseph Wafer was born in Enniscorthy in 1890 and by the time of the Rising was married and living in North Dublin. He was a captain in the 2nd Dublin Battalion and was killed in the Hibernian Bank at the corner of Sackville and Lower Abbey Street. His body was consumed in the fire that engulfed the building.

Eason & Sons

The founder of Ireland's leading stationers, Charles Eason, was an Englishman, born on 11th May 1823 in Yeovil, Somerset. In 1844 he was working in a bookshop in London and in 1850 he was made manager of the W.H. Smith bookstall at Victoria Station, London. The following year he married Caroline Binks. A man of strong principles he came to the attention of Smith who offered him the post of manager of the Dublin office. In two years he had reorganised it and was employing 23 staff. In 1868 he opened the Belfast branch. When in 1886 Eason went to London with an offer to buy the Irish business of Smith's, Eason had his son Charles Junior by his side. In 1896 Charles Senior died in an accident, leaving his son in sole control. Like most retailers in central Dublin Eason took a blow, their Abbey Street branch all but totally destroyed in the Easter Rising. Though at times the business has struggled it has continued to grow and now has branches in every major town in Ireland selling more than just stationery goods.

CHARLES EASON
1823-1899

**This is a portrait of the Englishman who founded the
company of the same name.**

Eason had for some time sold their own brand of postcards under the name of Signal Series (also used by W.H. Smith) identified by the E&S Ltd. DUB seen in the trademark shield printed on the back of each postcard. These cards were printed in Germany as were many postcards at this time. Many of their later postcards just bore the wording "E&S Ltd Dublin". The Eason issues of Rising postcards is strongly linked to the *Daily Sketch* unnumbered issues, the thirteen views being identical as are the captions. The only visible difference is on the back of the card which clearly states Copyright. Printed by the *Daily Sketch* for Messrs. Eason & Sons Ltd., Dublin.

Fergus O'Connor

On Monday 15th May 1916 Fergus O'Connor was sentenced to ten years, remitted to three, for his part in the Rising and was sent to Lewes where according to Robert Brennan's book *Allegiance* he was the joker in the jail. It was whilst in prison that he sent his mother a St. Patrick's Day letter. On his return to civilian life he set about building up his business from his premises at 44 Eccles Street. He produced a stream of postcard and other related material with a strong Nationalistic theme. Many of his postcards have woven into their design the colours of the Irish Tricolour.

Left: Keep your Colours Flying. This postcard, that is slightly larger than the average of the series, depicts the Irish tricolour blowing in the breeze with the legend in both Gaelic and English. The design was issued as a St. Patrick's Day postcard with the wording 'Greeting for St. Patrick's Day' across the top of the card.

Right: James Connolly. This is just one in a series of postcards depicting portraits of the executed leaders of the Rising.

Gaelic Press

During the Rising, Patrick Pearse wanted a newspaper printed for propaganda purposes so he turned to Joseph Michael Stanley who commandeered O'Keeffe's Printing Works in Halston Street to print *Irish War News*. Stanley was born in Clogerhead in Co. Louth. In 1913 he bought a struggling printing works and about this time he also became involved with the burgeoning Nationalist movement. His print shop at 21 Upper Liffey Street was raided on 24th March 1916 and the presses confiscated. For his actions during the Rising he was eventually sent to Frongoch where he wrote poetry and songs and was part of the entertainment committee. He was also a hut commander who together with other hut commanders were court martialled and sentenced to 28 days bread and water but were released after six days. In 1917 he renamed his company The Gaelic Press. His premises were subsequently subjected to several police raids. In 1919 he moved to Drogheda where he opened a cinema and the same year opened another in Dundalk. In 1920 he was elected to Louth County Council. In 1921, back in Dublin, he restarted The Gaelic Press. Eight years later he took up the post of sub-editor at the *Daily Mail* in London. In 1936 he returned to Drogheda and was the owner of the *Drogheda Argus and Advertiser*. Joseph Michael Stanley died in hospital in Drogheda in 1950.

The Gaelic Press was a publisher of truly political postcards. The designs depicted in their postcards spoke the message more so than the captions.

PULLING TOGETHER

This postcard depicts the boat Irish Nationality under the Catholic Church pilot hopefully pulling together. The boat is powered by the oars of all the political parties. The rowers would appear to be prominent Nationalists. Collins in the front row is in military uniform, with perhaps Timothy Healy on his left. Behind him is Griffith who has Joe Devlin pulling alongside of him and behind Devlin is Count Plunkett. Perhaps this design is meant to depict the Irish Delegation to the Independence Negotiations (in which case the person I believe to be Devlin is incorrect).

This plain postcard bears the words in Gaelic "Sinn Fein Forever".

John Bull:—"I'd like to, but———!"

Poor dithering John Bull has a dilemma. He is ready to use his gun on Ireland and the English press in the form of some creature is urging him to do so but he is rightly afraid of the consequences of his actions.

Hely's

In the *Dublin Gazetteer* of 1846 is an entry for Edward Hely & Co. of 12 Ormond Quay Lower as a manufacturer of paper, account books, stationer, engraver, and printer. By 1852 Charles Hely was in charge of the company and resided at 17 Dame Street. More change occurred when in 1880 the name became Hely, Charles Benden, Son & Co. Nine years later, with a move to 28 Dame Street, there was another name change, this time to Hely, Son & Co. The company was growing rapidly and in 1898 it purchased Nos. 27, 29 and 30 Dame Street and shortened the name to Hely's. This same year the first use of the name Acme Works appears as Printing and Binding Works, Dame Lane.

In March 1922 Hely's submitted essays for postage stamps to the new Provisional Government, but their design of a winged female set against a setting sun was not taken up. By 1930 the Acme Works had an extra site in Dame Court and the company was also selling fancy goods and sports merchandise. In 1940 they had a factory at East Wall producing packaging, paper bags, account books and colour printing. In 1960 the Acme works was closed and in 1965 Hely's amalgamated with another famous Dublin printers, Thom, to form Hely Thom Ltd., with a head office at 33 Botanic Works, George's Hill. In 1969 the site at Dame Street was closed, the company's name was changed to Helicon and it was bought by the Jefferson Smurfit Group.

There are eighteen known Rising views issued by Hely, all nice clean photographs with a white band at the base which carries the caption. There are, however, variations within these views. One of the views, of "Armoured Motor Car in Bachelor's Walk" is published in two formats, one full card and the other with white bands down the sides. Two of the views which are identical have different captions and in reverse there are two different views that share the one caption. One of the views was printed in two editions. Not to miss out on any sales opportunities, Hely issued a postcard on Michael Collins, to my knowledge the only Rising personality postcard they issued.

After the Insurrection.—Sackville Street. The D.B.C., a picturesque ruin.

A Hely's card with the odd caption "a picturesque ruin".

Keohan

Edmond Keohan was a famous photographer in Dungarvan who came from Tramore in the 1870s and opened a sweet shop at 17 Main Street. In 1880 he started his photography business, specialising in portraits and views of the town and the surrounding district. The shop grew into a newsagents and auctioneer office and in 1924 his book *Illustrated History of Dungarvan* was published by Edward Brennan & Co. of Dungarvan. The business closed in the 1970s. Keohan's postcards may have been printed by Edward Brennan & Co.

This, the usual portrait of O'Rahilly, was used by all the publishers.

K. Ltd

A small publisher that produced these cards (below) of Collins and Terence MacSwiney. I believe that the company also published postcards of other Nationalist leaders.

Michael Collins, T.D.

Michael Collins T.D. This portrait of Collins shows him sporting a moustache which he had when he went to London for the Peace talks.

TERENCE MacSWINEY. M.I.P. Lord Mayor Of Cork.

Terence MacSwiney M.I.P., Lord Mayor of Cork. A smart looking MacSwiney who became Lord Mayor after his friend and predecessor Tomás MacCurtain was killed by British soldiers. I believe M.I.P. stands for 'Murdered in Prison'.

Marshall Keene & Co. Hove, Sussex

This company were photographers and printers at 95 Portland Road, Hove, and also had a branch in London. They specialised in producing cards of schools and institutions. They opened for business in the mid 1920s sharing a premises with Thomas Dunkerton who was an established photographer.

Sackville Street after the conflict. This is one of the few fully coloured postcards of the aftermath of the Rising. This identical view was used in 1966 as part of the set of postcards issued to commemorate the 50th Anniversary of the Rising published by Irish Art Publications. I find it surprising that a company in England should issue a card on the Rising possibly ten or more years after the event.

Powell Press

Since 1884, the year in which the first patent was taken out for a Linotype printing machine, there has always been a printer at 22 Parliament Street and the name Powell has always been included in the company name. The name E. Powell only lasted for seven years during which time the company were printers to the British Army. Then, with a change of name to Edward Powell, trading continued for the next thirteen years from 1892 until 1905. John A. Powell carried on the business until 1913. In 1914 the company was depersonalised and took on the name it is known by today, Powell Press. In 1958 the owner of the company was, I believe, Mr. Michael Branagan. The company ceased trading exactly 100 years after it was founded in 1984.

Though the Powell Press, like most postcard publishers, is no longer in existence the company left behind a legacy that no other publisher has been able to match. Curran were the only company that came anywhere near to matching Powell. The range of the personalities they issued in postcard form covers the famous to the not so famous. They are to my knowledge the only company to issue cards of Richard O'Carroll, Con Keating and John F. McEntee amongst others. Their shamrock card of the Enniscorthy leaders was never copied by any other. They also produced what I believe was a second edition of postcards. The first edition of the cards are all printed with an italicised top caption: *IRISH REBELLION, MAY, 1916*; the other edition's top caption is printed as IRISH REBELLION, MAY, 1916. In this second edition there are several portraits taken from the first edition. Like other publishers they use May in their caption for the date of the Rising. Perhaps the most remarkable item produced by Powell was not a postcard but a poster. Powell produced three different posters that displayed their postcards. At this time these posters could easily have been considered as provocative or subversive by the authorities who perhaps decided not to take action as this might cause them more problems.

Right: This is believed to be a first edition of this Henry O'Hanrahan postcard. The caption above the portrait is in italics which is the form of most of the Powell Press postcards.

Below right: This I believe is a second edition of the previous card. The caption above the portrait uses a bolder block typeface whilst the lower caption is in a larger and in some cases bolder typeface.

Below: A Powell Press poster. Just one of the three posters issued by Powell to advertise their postcards.

HENRY O'HANRAHAN
(Brother of Michael O'Hanrahan, who was Executed),
Sentenced to Penal Servitude.

IRISH REBELLION, MAY, 1916.

IRISH REPUBLICAN ARMY
Leaders in the Insurrection, May, 1916

HENRY O'HANRAHAN
(Brother of Michael O'Hanrahan, who was Executed),
Sentenced to Penal Servitude.

Rotary Press E.C.

The title above is the name that appears on the front of the postcards that were issued by the Rotary Photographic Company Limited that took their name from the presses that produced their vast range of postcards. The E.C. is the postal district of London, East Central.

It was during the "Golden Age" of postcards that the company was formed at 23 Moorfields, London in 1901. The company had set their sights too low as within a year they had to move to larger premises at 14 New Union Street. Yet again such was the growth of the business that another move was necessitated in 1904 to 12 New Union Street, where the business was now accommodated in a six storey building that included offices and showrooms. Eventually the production of the postcards was moved to a factory in West Drayton, Middlesex for by now they had become one of the country's major publishers of postcards. The range of topics they produced included actors, actresses, scenes from plays, royalty, sportsmen, statesmen and personalities of the art world and by 1904 the company was printing three million postcards a year. They did not lag behind in the field of novelty postcards. The range now extended to midget postcards, bookmark cards, stereoscopic cards, diamond shaped and 'jewelled' and beaded cards. Special sets of six postcards, depicting scenes from most of the productions from the London theatre, were issued. In 1908 the Marlborough Art Miniatures Series was produced which, together with the Burlington Art Miniatures Series, contained 240 postcards. In 1902, it was claimed, they produced the first New Year's Day card. By 1910 their offices at New Union Street were disposed of and the company moved to several sites in the City of London, and by 1918 they were to be found at 8 Finsbury Square. The Rotary Photographic Co. (1917) Ltd. was founded to take over the assets of the old company and now moved the whole company to West Drayton. Though still involved in photographic work the company ceased producing postcards in 1945.

Rotary only produced seven postcards of the Rising that were numbered 6719-7 to 6719-13 from five views, all of which are matt finished photographic cards.

The obligatory view of Liberty Hall produced by all publishers: Liberty Hall with bemused Dubliners surveying a familiar building.

6719—7   THE SINN FEIN REVOLT IN DUBLIN.   ROTARY PHOTO. E.C.
THE METROPOLE HOTEL, POST OFFICE AND NELSON COLUMN

This is a good general view of Sackville Street with Nelson Pillar, not Column as stated in the caption.

Sandridge

To my knowledge the only Rising postcard this firm produced is that of Casement and Montieth.

The Landing of Roger Casement and Capt. Monteith on the Coast of Kerry.   [Copyright

This stylised view does not include Bailey who also landed with them and is a photomontage.

Shamrock Card Co.

The Shamrock Card Co. is an interesting case. Other publishers used Valentine's views and published them using their own imprints. Shamrock took Coleman's views and published under their name, although it may be that Coleman, wishing to sell their postcards, needed to create a separate company and chose a traditional name like Shamrock.

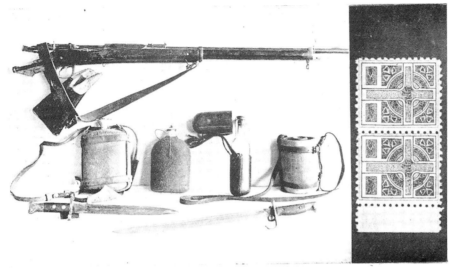

SINN FEIN REVOLT.
Arms and Equipment.

Stamp issued.

Sibley

Sibley titled themselves as Sibley, Booksellers and Stationer, Grafton Street, Dublin and were at No. 51. Like many other small businesses they published, under their own imprint, three of Valentine's views.

Grafton Street Dublin.

This coloured postcard published by Lawrence of Dublin shows the Location of Sibley's shop in Grafton Street, *c*.1910. The two gentlemen, one of whom is wearing the light coloured jacket, are standing outside Sibley & Co. The card enlarged makes their shop facia readable and states that they sell "Fountain & Stylographic Pens".

Tarlton

Tarlton Publishing Co. had its offices right in the middle of the Rising at 52 Middle Abbey Street where they remained until 1921. In the main they produced portraits of the leading protagonists using the Keogh Brothers' portraits as their source.

This is the only postcard that I know of, other than the Valentine issues, that depict the events at Howth. The quarter views show the preparation and finally the achieved aim of Volunteers with rifles.

Left: **This is the normal portrait of the dark-eyed Ceannt and was from the Keogh Brothers studio.**
Right: **Constance is shown here embracing her new-found Irish heritage wearing a Celtic sash broach.**

Valentine

Sinn Fein Rebellion, 1916.
Hotel Metropole and
Post Office, Dublin.

James Valentine was the founder of the company whose trade mark "Famous Through The World" written through twin globes became so recognisable to tourists and collectors alike.

Valentine was a Scot, born in Dundee in 1815. He studied in Edinburgh as a portrait painter but at the age of 17 he was forced to give up his ambitions and join the family business that made woodblock engraving for printing linen patterns. Here he made changes to the company, including the name which now became James Valentine & Son, Engravers and Printers. By 1840 the company was producing local scenes and illustrating envelopes with religious and moral themes. James started photographic experiments and by 1850 became so engrossed he went to Paris to study. By 1856 he had opened a photographic studio in Murraygate in Dundee and two years later decided to move to 23 High Street. In 1868 Queen Victoria bestowed upon the company the Royal Warrant as Photographer to the Queen for the 40 Scottish scenes she commissioned. James Valentine's sons, William and George, joined their father in the business and extended their series of photographic views to cover the whole of Great Britain. The amount of views became so vast that an identification system was set up. Thus all the Valentine views were prefixed with a "JV" number. It was not until 1897 that the company produced its first postcard and in 1904 *The Postcard Connoisseur* praised Valentine as "one of the largest publishers of photographic views of the world". At the 1908 Franco-British Exhibition held in London they won an award for their colour and photographic printing and two years later at the Brussels Exhibition they won similar awards. At the outbreak of the First World War the company had offices in Canada, South Africa, America, Australia and Scandinavia. In Ireland they had offices at 44 William Street, Dublin. They also had four factories and employed more than 600 workers in Ireland. In 1911 they contracted Mabel Lucie Attwell whose drawings of children were sold by the company for over 50 years. With the "Golden Age of Postcards" fast waning they started producing greetings cards whilst maintaining postcard production. In 1963 the company was taken over by John Waddington Ltd. who in turn sold it on to Hallmark Cards. Despite all these changes Valentine still remain in Dundee where their factory complex of 28,000 square feet overlooks the Kingsway. Some of the Valentine archives are now in the safe keeping of St. Andrews University, Fife who sadly only have eight registered Valentine views of the Rising on their register.

As befits one of the world's leading postcard producers, Valentine published more postcard views of the Easter Rising than any other publisher. Their views graphically display the destructive events of that week. Many of the views feature the central areas of Dublin, but other events were covered such as the arrest of McBride and Markievicz, Volunteers parading through the streets, the Citizen Army on the roof of Liberty Hall, priests being searched by soldiers, priests at the bedside of the wounded and visitors to a prison being searched. These all tell the story of the Rising more so perhaps than ruined buildings.

Their Collotype views added new scenes that were more interesting than the original issues and Valentine were the only publisher to produce coloured views of the Rising. From their library of views the "Before and After" series drew one's attention to how it was and the reality of how it was now.

Valentine used an ordinary view card of Sackville Street and by adding the wording "As it was before the Sinn Fein Rebellion" turned it into a Rising postcard. Some of the views have in the opinion of the Valentine's artistic director been improved with the addition of imposed flames and persons.

And finally the backs of their cards have added another puzzlement to their postcards. On the back of each postcard is a stamp box – the preferred positioning for stamps by the Post Office. Cards with the same view on the front often had different numbers ranging from 6, 7, 8.1, 8.2, 9.1, 9.2, 20.1 and 22.2 printed in the stamp box. Several theories have been put forward, a date code being the obvious one, but none seem to solve the mystery.

Sackville Street, Dublin (As it was before Sinn Fein Rebellion, 1916

This is an example of a view card turned into a Rising card. The caption is now printed in red, it has extra words "As it was" and finally the bracket is missing from the end of the caption. This particular copy of this card has an ink cross over Nelson's Pillar. Turn the card and the message reads: "Dear Wife this is a postcard where a man killed himself by throwing himself from the top of this Pillar it is Nelson and it is 300 feet high you might have seen the accident in the paper he belongs to England". On Friday 20th July 1917 the *Dublin Evening Mail* headed one of its leader columns TRAGEDY telling of a SOLDIER'S LEAP TO DEATH and Pathetic Farewell Message to His Wife. It then reported on the soldier's inquest. Other facts to emerge from the inquest was that the dead man Clarence C. Caldwell was 31 and had lived at 1 Stephen Street, Wolverhampton. He had been discharged from the Royal Field Artillery the previous year. The suicide happened at 2 p.m. and the man was taken to Gervis Street Hospital in a "motor delivery van" belonging to Messrs Rosa & Co. of Great Britain Street. It also stated that the Pillar was 120ft tall. What both the card writer and the newspaper got wrong was that Nelson's Pillar, before being blown up by the I.R.A. in 1966 was not 300ft nor 120ft tall but 134ft tall.

J. J. Walsh

James Joseph Walsh was born on 20th February 1880 near Bandon in Co. Cork. After little schooling he passed the postal service exam, spending three years in London in the service. Returning to Cork he worked at the Cork International Exhibition and helped to organise the Tailteann Games and was also an active member of the G.A.A. During the Easter Rising he fought in the G.P.O. and was sentenced to death, commuted to ten years imprisonment. He was released in the general amnesty and won the seat of Cork City as a Sinn Fein candidate. He was a member of the first Dail for which he was arrested and only released in 1921. He supported the Treaty and from 1922-24 was Postmaster General and again held the post when it became the Department of Posts and Telegraphs. He retained his seat in all elections until 1927 when he retired from politics. He was almost arrested for his Fascist and anti-Semitic views during the Second World War and died on 30th November 1948.

Arthur Griffith T.D.,

J. J. WALSH

Arthur Griffith T.D. This postcard shows an ageing Griffith. His life's work for the founding of an Irish state finally took its toll on him.

F. W. Woolworth & Co. Ltd.

Woolworth did not print their own postcards but used views from Valentine and published them with their own imprint. This postcard was published in black and white and in colour.

Before and After. Woolworth's cards can be identified by a 'W' enclosed in a diamond (their trade mark) on the back of the card.

Chapter 15: Souvenir Booklets

Today most national and international events are available to buy in some digital format for the public to keep as a souvenir. The main souvenirs of the Easter Rising were postcards. There were also a plethora of books on the subject, many of which went into the details of the Rising. Also available was a selection of souvenir booklets that in the main were a pictorial record of the event. These booklets were published by several publishers of postcards: Eason, Hely and Baird.

Dublin and the "Sinn Fein Rising"

This booklet was published by Wilson Hartnell & Co. Dublin and sold for 9d. The vignette in the centre of the cover shows the ruins all around O'Connell's statue and is not unfairly titled as "YPRES ON THE LIFFEY". The booklet of 28 pages contains 56 illustrations of various shapes and sizes, some of which were used as postcards of the Rising. Various portraits of those executed are shown, together with many scenes of the destroyed city. The first part of the booklet is full of illustrations, each with a caption beneath it, whilst the last part has text describing the events of the Rising. The illustrations are attributed in most cases and rely on the photographs of Valentine, Lawrence, Keogh Bros., Chancellor, Lafayette and T. W. Murphy. An interesting feature of this publication is the reproduction of *The Irish War News* which was stapled into the centre of it. The publishers, not wishing to miss an opportunity, have six pages of adverts. The inside cover carries a full page advert for E & J BURKES Old Dublin Whiskey. Other pages have box adverts for the Gresham, Hammam, and Jury's Hotels. There is even an advert for Hopkins and Hopkins whose premises were totally destroyed during the Rising. At ninepence this booklet was one of the more expensive publications available. This booklet was also published with a buff coloured cover and with a different title THE REBELLION in DUBLIN, April 1916. These are probably reprints.

This very battered copy is intact, but much the worst for wear.

It is a puzzle why Chancellor, who had their main studios at the corner of Sackville Street and Bachelors Walk, and who produced high quality photographs of the Rising that are used in many of these booklets never published postcards themselves or had their views published as postcards.

The "Sinn Fein" Revolt Illustrated

This booklet was printed and published by Hely at their Acme Works in Dame Street, Dublin. The view on the cover shows a peaceful O'Connell Bridge and Sackville Street which changes as soon as the cover is turned. The first photograph is a panoramic view of a devastated Dublin that is slowly trying to return to normal, photographed by Mr. Geo. D. Gray, Assistant Engineer, Dublin Corporation.

The inside cover carries an advert for SANDERSONS Motor Works at 20 Up. Dorset St. Dublin. The eighteen pages contain 69 illustrations of varying shapes and sizes, one of which is the ruined shop of Eason & Sons in Middle Abbey Street. Many of the illustrations were also published as Hely postcards. There is plenty of text, not all of which is accurate. "Edward de Valera. Born in Galway…" is perhaps one of the most significant incorrect statements. At the time there must have been many rumours and half truths that in the rush to print were not verified. How wise it is to be after an event. The words for this booklet were supplied by J.W.M. whoever he or she was. The photographs are laid out in a chronological order. The final words of the book quote an anonymous Sherwood Forester who remarked during the Rising "Queer people, you Irish, some of you shot us in the back while others stuff us with refreshment and smother us with kindness".

The portraits of the executed are all in oval frames and there are reproductions of documents and several interesting military views. The photographs are attributed to Keogh Bros., College Studios and Mr. T. W. Murphy. Like other publications this one has four full pages of adverts apart from the inside cover and include one for Clery announcing that temporary premises have been secured at Earl Place. This booklet differs from all others in that no price is shown on the cover.

Battered but not bowed is probably the best way to describe this copy of Hely's booklet. It is still in one piece though that piece is a little worn.

1916 The Sinn Fein Rebellion &
Dublin After the Six Days Insurrection

These two booklets pose a conundrum as both books are identical in size, have the same colour cover, contain the same text and photographs, and sold for the same price, 7d. *1916 The Sinn Fein Rebellion* has at the right hand corner of the back cover a bird design reminiscent of an eagle or a phoenix and within it a circle which contains the name W&G Baird Ltd. and a lower circle with Belfast in it. The other booklet, *Dublin After the Six Day Insurrection*, has all the physical features of the previous booklet except that the front cover has more information on it. Most of all Mr. T. W. Murphy gets the recognition he deserves, his name on the front cover and we also learn he was the sub-editor of *The Motor News*. The cover also clearly gives the publisher's name as Mecredy, Percy & Co. Ltd. 11 & 12 Findlater Place, Upper Sackville Street. The heading on this cover states that this publication has been PASSED FOR TRANSMISSION ABROAD BY THE OFFICAL PRESS BUREAU. The other difference is that the back cover has an advert for another Mecredy and Percy publication, *Bulls and Blunders* by J.C. Percy, described as 'A TYPICAL IRISH BOOK' and priced at 1s. (shilling). These are the only differences between the two publications.

The grey cover has a Celtic style design on the waffle effect grey. This booklet is also known to have been published with a red cover.

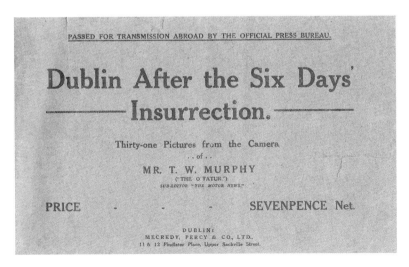

The plain design of this booklet cover gives the buyer all the information about the product.

As to the publications themselves they contain 31 photographs, all of which have a caption of one line in upper case and eight that have an extra line of caption in lower case. The views are of destruction with the exception of the last two. Some of the views show more clearly the condition that Dublin was left in at the end of the Rising and several were reproduced by Baird, Hely, and Coleman in postcard form. There is only one page of text, on the first page of the booklet. And so to the conundrum: did Baird print the booklet, which they were very capable of doing so and then lease it to Mecredy & Percy or, did Mecredy & Percy, whom I know only as publishers, get the booklet printed and leased it to Baird? I rather favour the first of these options.

The Rebellion in Dublin, April 1916

At the time of the Rising Eason & Son had a network of shops across the country, making it one of the few postcard publishing companies working nationally. It had produced its own products for some years, so its Rising postcards were not its first venture into this market. A natural progression from the postcards would be a booklet on the Rising. They published two issues of their booklet, a small edition and a large edition. The small edition contained thirteen pages and the larger contained eighteen pages. The small edition sold for 6d and the larger for 1s. Both editions followed the same format. The cover for the booklets was printed on a thick dark brown paper and on it was a drawing in black ink of the Customs House, together with the title and the price. On the back cover were the words Eason & Son, Ltd. Dublin and Belfast enclosed in an orange lined rectangle. The first page of the booklet contained a brief description of the Rising and was printed on a strong tan coloured paper similar to the cover but of a thinner gauge. The remainder of the pages are coloured a dark tan and contain one image per page. Of the views shown one is by Lafayette, one by Baird, two by Keogh Bros., five by Chancellor and four unattributed. The first two pages contain images of Pearse, Connolly, Clarke, MacDonagh and McBride together with a Republican "stamp", which was in fact a Sinn Fein propaganda label. All the other views are of destruction with the exception of the last one which is of the Royal College of Surgeons. All the views are printed in sepia. The views were printed and then set into the page surrounded by a black border. The pages were stapled together and then drilled with the cover and strung together.

All of the above applies to the larger edition which had five extra views, all of destruction. There was another edition published by Eason & Son that was identical to the small edition but was priced at 7d. It is unknown why the price was increased from 6d to 7d but it could be that the booklet proved so popular that they increased the price to make extra profit. Or it may have been that they were losing money on the small edition and needed to recoup the loss.

THE REBELLION IN DUBLIN April 1916. The cover shows a nice sketch of the Customs House and on the left can be seen the string that ties the item together. It may be that the design used the Custom House because it was the only iconic building left standing in Dublin. The covers for all three editions are identical to the one shown apart from the change of price.